"Isaac Serrano's *When [Life Feels Empty* is a timely] work that challenges us to reexamine the roots of our discontent and rediscover what truly sustains a meaningful life. This book not only illuminates the depth of our modern struggles but also offers a hopeful, practical pathway to a life marked by purpose and fulfillment. It's a call to look upward—to see beyond the temporary and to seek what is eternal. It is a must-read for anyone yearning to experience true meaning amid life's uncertainties."
Charles J. Conniry Jr., president of Western Seminary

"In an age that trades transcendence for transactions and mystery for materialism, Isaac Serrano unearths the ancient practices that have long anchored humanity. With a surgeon's precision and a shepherd's heart, he exposes the void in our modern soul and offers timeless remedies to weave us back into God's grand narrative. *When Life Feels Empty* doesn't just reveal the ache in our culture—it heals it, turning hevel into hallelujah."
Leonard Sweet, author of *Decoding the Divine* and proprietor of Sanctuary Seaside advance center

"We live in an age of perpetual dissatisfaction. What 'is' always feels disappointing when compared with what 'could be,' and we find ourselves exhausted on the hedonic treadmill, always chasing, never arriving. But the answer to our angst is found in what 'always has been.' With cultural precision and pastoral wisdom, Isaac Serrano guides us across our history as the people of God and leads us into a future of meaning, purpose, and joy. For any and all seeking a life of fulfillment, *When Life Feels Empty* is the guidebook you've been searching for."
Jay Y. Kim, pastor and author of *Analog Christian*

"The gravitational pull of this book, from its opening pages, draws us through a clear-eyed view of the despair of our world into a hope that can only emerge from a deep reckoning of truth. With philosophical reasoning, theological insights, and compelling wisdom, Isaac Serrano leaves us looking into the face of a good and grand God."
Nancy Ortberg, CEO of Transforming the Bay with Christ

"Isaac Serrano's very lively, readable volume is a marvelous contemporary application of the book of Ecclesiastes, whose enduring value is reinforced yet again. Serrano's life experience, keen pastoral insights, and pointed practical engagement with real issues in our culture make this a penetrating, thought-provoking work on life's meaning for our day and age."
Paul Copan, Pledger Family Chair of Philosophy and Ethics at Palm Beach Atlantic University and author of *A Little Book for New Philosophers*

"There doesn't seem to be a more intense time period where so many are disillusioned, tired, emotionally overloaded, and wondering what life is really about. It feels like it is easier to just give up thinking about it and hope that somehow change will happen to bring us movement into something more than we are currently experiencing. *When Life Feels Empty* is a guide for that change to happen and gives us tangible ways to move from emptiness to meaning and purpose the way we are meant to experience them."

Dan Kimball, author of *How (Not) to Read the Bible* and vice president of Western Seminary

When Life Feels Empty

7 Ancient Practices to Cultivate Meaning

ISAAC SERRANO

ivp

An imprint of InterVarsity Press
Downers Grove, Illinois

InterVarsity Press
P.O. Box 1400 | Downers Grove, IL 60515-1426
ivpress.com | email@ivpress.com

©2025 by Joseph Isaac Serrano

All rights reserved. No part of this book may be reproduced in any form without written permission from InterVarsity Press.

InterVarsity Press® is the publishing division of InterVarsity Christian Fellowship/USA®. For more information, visit intervarsity.org.

Scripture quotations, unless otherwise noted, are from The Holy Bible, English Standard Version. ESV© Text Edition: 2016. Copyright © 2001 by Crossway Bibles, a publishing ministry of Good News Publishers. Used by permission. All rights reserved.

While any stories in this book are true, some names and identifying information may have been changed to protect the privacy of individuals.

The Veiled Virgin, photo by Shhewitt, Creative Commons license / Wikimedia Commons

The publisher cannot verify the accuracy or functionality of website URLs used in this book beyond the date of publication.

Cover design: Faceout Studio, Spencer Fuller
Interior design: Jeanna Wiggins

ISBN 978-1-5140-1063-1 (print) | ISBN 978-1-5140-1064-8 (digital)

Printed in the United States of America ♾

Library of Congress Cataloging-in-Publication Data
A catalog record for this book is available from the Library of Congress.

31 30 29 28 27 26 25 | 12 11 10 9 8 7 6 5 4 3 2 1

To the Serrano Six

In you I see the true, the good, and the beautiful.

Contents

PART 1: Signs and Symptoms

1. A Tragic Story / 3
2. Telos / 8
3. Hevel / 19
4. Truth, Goodness, Beauty / 28
5. Toddlers / 35
6. Zombies / 44
7. Religious Materialist / 51

PART 2: The Remedy—Belief and Embodiment
(The Wisdom of Our Ancestors)

8. To Know God / 61
9. Song / 67
10. Baptism / 77
11. Communion / 90
12. Thanksgiving / 103
13. Bible / 115
14. Church / 127
15. The Lord's Prayer / 142

PART 3: Practices and Patterns

16. Spirits / 153
17. The Stone and the Sculptor / 168

Notes / 179

Part 1

Signs and Symptoms

1

A Tragic Story

On September 18, 2010, thirty-five-year-old Mitchell Heisman walked onto a university campus and ended his life. The details of the event are haunting.

The location: the steps of Memorial Church at Harvard University. The building was originally constructed in memory of Harvard graduates lost in the Great War, the "War to End All Wars," World War I.

The time: eleven o'clock in the morning on the holiest day of the Jewish Calendar, Yom Kippur, the Day of Atonement. In Jewish Tradition, this is the climax of the year, the day when God looks at the sum total of sins committed by the nation and forgives them.

On sacred ground, and in sacred time, sacred life is lost.

Heisman left behind a suicide note, and this "note" may be unlike anything before it. It was over nineteen hundred pages, an amalgamation of ramblings and emotions, and yet at times, philosophical insight. In it he states, "Every word, every thought, and every emotion come back to one core problem: *life is meaningless.*"[1]

Heisman reflects on his dive into despair and pinpoints the precise moment his journey began. He writes, "The death of my father marked the beginning, or perhaps the acceleration, of a kind of moral collapse."[2] The death of an earthly father would ultimately lead this young Jewish man to reject any notion of a benevolent God above.

In losing one father, he lost two.

The loss of God and ultimately any form of reality above makes a life where no distinction between heaven and hell can be made. All becomes chaos, and all becomes purposeless. Heisman explains, "If there is no extant God and no extant gods, no good and no evil, no right and no wrong, no meaning and no purpose: if there are no values that are inherently valuable; no justice that is ultimately justifiable . . . then destruction is equal to creation; life is equal to death and death is equal to life."[3]

The world is a hell of a place to face without a father.

And this is the point where Heisman's story intersects with ours. And by "ours" I don't mean you or me, I mean all of us—the collective whole of our culture, because the signs that something is wrong are with us everywhere. The symptoms of our ailment are evident.

For two decades Americans have become more unhappy, more discontented, and more depressed than ever before. This is not just empty rhetoric; the research is clear. Suicide has gone up every year in nearly every state for the last two decades.[4] Anxiety is up. Loneliness is up. All around, misery is up.

Without a remedy for this, people are running to anything that will help them cope. In 2023 there were over one hundred thousand deaths due to drug overdoses.[5] This is more than five times the number just twenty years ago.[6] Half the country says they are lonely.[7] One in five young women practice self-harm.[8]

We are overeating, undereating, cutting, drinking, spending, popping, shooting, searching for anything that might help us face the emptiness before us.

Now, what is so bizarre about this is that as we become more unhappy and dissatisfied, we simultaneously participate in a greater and greater standard of living. The life we live is more comfortable than most people who have ever walked the earth could ever dream up.

Think about our standard of living for a moment. We walk into a grocery store and see more food in a single instance than some will ever see in their entire life. Think about the climate control we have at our fingertips. While we travel, if we feel the slightest degree of discomfort, we have the ability to fix it. If it gets just a bit too warm, we can flick a button and our car will begin to cool the entire vehicle. If we get too cold, we can heat it up.

And consider this: The water in our toilets is cleaner than the drinking water that millions of people have access to. We live in a comfort that our ancestors never dreamed of. Still, we are not happy. The standard of living goes up, yet our spirits go down.

So even though we experience the many benefits the modern world has afforded us, for many there is something that still does not feel right. Something is lurking deep in our gut. Despite living in the land of milk and honey, we can't shake the feeling that something is wrong at the center of it all. Like Heisman, we begin to contemplate ultimate things. Is it all meaningless? All without purpose? The possibility that our stories are authorless is frightening.

There are many opinions on the cause of our problem. Some will say it's social media. Others will point to Hollywood. For some, it's the breakdown of the family. Still others attribute it to failing schools and public education.

Certainly, these and many other factors are at play, but I'd like to talk about something deeper. Much deeper. *So deep* that we are nearly at the unconscious level, almost like the operating system of the mind. Because it is there, and precisely there, that something went very wrong.

CONFLICTING MESSAGES

Two messages currently broadcast around the clock in our culture. One message is loud, the other is softer. The loud message says, "You are a wonderful, amazing individual with purpose, meaning, and value. The world is before you, so make the most of every day and be the person you want to be!" This positive, uplifting message sits atop a metaphoric ten-story building. The softer message sits at the base—not as loud but foundational, holding up the entire building. It says, "You are a product of random chance. You are nothing more than neurons, chemicals, hormones, and atoms. You have no soul. There is nothing beyond this life. No heaven. No hell. No loving figure above."

Despite what is broadcast from the tenth floor, this foundation-level message speaks to the core of our being. It functions as an operating system. Our thoughts, feelings, and decisions are processed through it. Whether we like it or not, we live within the story it tells.

An experiment began roughly three hundred years ago in the modern world. The experiment sought to create a world divorced from God, religion, and anything other than the material world. In this endeavor, humans attempted to find ultimate meaning and purpose strictly from the physical world.

Despite the message that we tell ourselves—that we are special, unique, and have purpose—underneath that, at the foundation, at the operating system level, is the message that says we are alone in the universe. Our feet wander aimlessly without meaning on a planet that wanders aimlessly without meaning. We are here for a fleeting moment and then, death.

No matter how much we want to believe the message on the tenth floor, and no matter how much our pop songs, cultural slogans, and uplifting movies affirm that message, it is nonetheless built on a foundation that says otherwise. And we live within the confines of the narrative structure it gives us.

We want to believe in things like love, but however we may conceive of it, the foundational message says it does not exist. Love is just chemicals and hormones firing off in our body to create a social contract between two individuals so that they might propagate the herd. Integrity, honor, virtue . . . those are just terms we use to describe animal-like behaviors that benefit the tribe. We may assign meaning to all sorts of things in our lives, but make no mistake about it: things like integrity, honor, and virtue are not grounded in anything real. This foundational message is all-encompassing and incredibly powerful.

What is the result of this loss? We lack meaning and purpose, and the signs of our sickness are evident. The foundational message cannot bear the weight of the whole building, and it will collapse.

When Mitchell Heisman lost his father, the pillars that gave structure to his reality began to fall. The loss of father rendered life meaningless. We, too, have lost a father, and that can make life unbearable.

The world is a hell of a place to face without a father.

2

Telos

OKAY, I KNOW THAT WAS A BIT of a dark way to start a book that is supposed to help combat the feelings of emptiness, but the story embodies our situation quite well.

I serve as a pastor and teacher, and for the last two decades I have listened to both Christians and non-Christians express a common feeling—a feeling that something is missing from their lives. Most of the time, it's hard for people to pinpoint and even harder to articulate, but time and time again they say they have everything they need but nevertheless feel something lacking. There is an enduring sense that life is empty and without meaning and purpose. This feeling is especially pronounced with younger people, but I have seen it across the board. My hope is that whether you find yourself feeling this way or know others who have expressed similar sentiments and want to help them, this book will aid you.

To better understand our problem, the first question we should probably ask is, How did we get here? And by here, I mean a culture that believes there is nothing above. No heavenly Father, no God, no ultimate end goal, nothing to ground our feet in this ever-changing world. Because whether we like this story or not, this is now the default story our culture believes and the story we find ourselves living in.

You might push back and say, "I know plenty of people who believe in God," or maybe you are a person of faith yourself. But the fact remains: the ecosystem in which you live is an ecosystem that is thoroughly saturated in materialism. Materialism is the air you breathe.

I don't mean materialism in the sense that our culture is a greedy one fixated on acquiring material things (although that is probably true as well). The materialism I am referring to is the belief that the physical world is all that exists. This belief can come in a number of different forms and with different degrees of strength, but this basic definition should feel familiar.

In its strongest form, materialism says that there is no possibility for anything outside of the physical world. Everything that is real is that which can be observed in the physical world using physical senses, tools, and methods.

In its weakest form, materialism says something like, "It's certainly possible that things outside of our physical, observable universe exist, but if they do, they are not what is most important, and we have no way of knowing anyway. What is most important and most real are the things our five senses can detect. So, if there are such things as spiritual realities and you are inclined to believe in them, good for you."

If you are a religious person, the strong form says you are stupid or gullible, or both. The weak version smiles and says, "Oh, I didn't know you were religious. Well, I'm glad that works for you."

Does this sound familiar?

HAMBURGERS AND FRENCH FRIES

Have you ever eaten at In-N-Out Burger? If you haven't, they are a West Coast fast-food chain of legendary status. When people out of the area come to California where I live, they will often make a mandatory stop at In-N-Out Burger before they leave. One thing you need to know is that there is a unique aroma that fills the restaurant. In fact, you can smell it merely driving by. Fans of the restaurant love the smell and anticipate it when they go. The exact source of the unique aroma is a bit of a mystery . . . some say it's the onions, others say it's the spread on the burger, others claim it's the fries.

Now, imagine you work long hours every day at In-N-Out Burger. Just being in that space for the day does something to you and the clothes you wear. You sort of just start smelling like In-N-Out Burger. Even when you leave the restaurant and go home, your family smells In-N-Out when you walk in. You may hate In-N-Out and despise the taste of their food; you may even vow in your heart to never eat an In-N-Out Burger again . . . it doesn't matter. If you work at In-N-Out, you will smell like In-N-Out.[1]

I came across a Reddit forum post titled "Is it just me or can you guys still 'smell' in-n-out hours after working?"[2] Here are a few of the responses:

"Even after showering, I think maybe there's oils or something in my nose that I inhaled. Smells like a mix of onions and fried mustard."

"I used to work fries all day Saturday and Sunday. If I went out after, I was eighteen at the time, no matter how hard I scrubbed I would smell like fries. It was kinda bad but girls would be like 'you smell like hash browns!!'"

"I completely shower and change when I get home from work. I used to go to class right after work in my whites until people started mentioning I smell like burgers and onions lol."

Materialism works in a similar matter. It's the building that we work in. It's the air we breathe. And no matter how hard we try to resist, we live inside the ecosystem that it has created.

In this way, materialism functions as a dominant story. Stories like these are all encompassing and shape how you see the world. These types of stories are so powerful that you don't believe them; rather, by default, you live inside of them.

Imagine for a moment that you lived two thousand years ago in a city named Ephesus. Ephesus was located in a region called Asia

Minor, near the eastern edge of the Roman Empire. If you lived in first-century Ephesus, everything in your community reinforced the dominant story the culture was telling. This was a story that said the gods and goddesses ruled the day.

In Ephesus, there was a massive temple dedicated to Artemis. It was one of the Seven Wonders of the Ancient World. No matter where you stood in Ephesus, its structure imposed itself upon you. You could not escape it. The temple sat on an elevated plateau so it could loom over the city. Its height then extended further with one hundred and twenty-seven columns, each sixty feet in height.[3] Artemis was an ever-present reality.

In Ephesus, you lived inside the ecosystem created by the story of the gods and goddesses. Whether you liked it or not, if you took a stroll down the streets of Ephesus, you breathed the air of the gods. And because of this, if you were born in Ephesus in the first century, you sort of just absorbed belief in the gods.

Now let's return to today. We also absorb beliefs from the time we live in. It's easy to see how this took place in other older cultures and it's also easy to forget it is true of our own. C. S. Lewis reminds us, "Our own age is also 'a period,' and certainly has, like all periods, its own characteristic illusions. They are likeliest to lurk in those widespread assumptions which are so ingrained in the age that no one dares to attack or feels it necessary to defend them."[4] Materialism is the story of our time, and we all, like people living in Ephesus two thousand years ago, have absorbed the tenets of that story to different degrees. Since the day you were born you have been living in the world that materialism is creating, and it is now the ever-present reality. Even someone raised in the Christian faith is also someone who is simultaneously raised in materialism.

And just like working at In-N-Out or living in Ephesus, there is no escape from this. All cultures and peoples have stories that we see the world through. It is in and through these stories that we make sense of our lives and the world around us. These stories answer life's biggest and toughest questions. They tell us who we are and where we come from; they give us our meaning and purpose. They give us a "why" to life. The massive problem is that the materialist story is insufficient in offering answers to the deepest questions of life: *Who am I? Where am I going? For what reason do I exist? What is the meaning of it all?* Humans are reduced to a machinery of carbon, neurons, and synapses, and meaning is lost as we wander without aim.

UNCHARTED TERRITORY

This materialist way of looking at the world is, from a historical viewpoint, new. Sure, you can find groups dabbling with different forms of nontheism or materialism throughout history, but there has never been an entire culture that has so thoroughly adopted materialism other than our current, modern Western culture. Stepping into this disenchanted and godless story is to step into a brave new world of uncharted territory.

For many, this new world was going to produce a world of happiness, abundance, and satisfaction the world had not yet seen. We were going to throw off the shackles of tyrannical gods and religious systems. We were saying goodbye to the fairy tales, the myths, the hocus-pocus that only unenlightened, uneducated, and unscientific-minded people gullibly gobbled up. Our eyes were finally open and we could see the fruit for what it was, a fruit good and pleasing to the eye and worthy of taking. Without the tyrant above looking down on us, demanding we create the world that he wanted, we could say goodbye to that demanding father and create the world *we* wanted. After wandering around and being lost in the wilderness of religion, we could now enter a godless promised land.

Or at least that's what we told ourselves.

But what happened when we finally arrived in this promised land? Did life become better? The loss of God was like a giant meteor hitting earth. If you survived the impact, then there were still a host of effects after the initial impact that you would have to live with.

We are living in the aftermath of that great impact. The Western world exiled God and thought if we could survive the initial impact, then we would be able to rebuild and create a world greater than the previous one. However, the effects of the initial impact were much greater than expected. We thought we could build again, but we lost not only the tools but also the know-how and vocabulary to do so.

How were we to rebuild without the materials that belief in God gave us? How were we to understand morality, ethics, beauty, love, hate, mercy, and justice if not grounded on some type of foundation? How could we bear the harsh reality of pain and suffering without the floor that gave us the surface to stand on? To whom or where could we look for purpose and direction? To what or to whom could we turn toward to find fullness rather than emptiness? In losing God, we lost the building blocks necessary to construct a meaningful life.

One of those building blocks was one presupposed in our ancestors' understanding of the world. This building block was the ground used as a foundation to build meaning on. It is so important that when lacking, the human story becomes unbearable. It was known across cultures but was articulated by the ancient Greeks with the word *telos*.

Telos is a word that can be translated and employed in several ways, but contained in the word is an understanding of aim, direction, or end goal. What is the telos of an acorn? To become an oak tree. What is the telos of the tadpole? To become a frog. When people ask, "What is the meaning of life?" this is often what they are thinking about. What is the telos of my life? Do I matter? What is the point and purpose of it all?

In the materialist story, we live and breathe and die in a world without telos. We live in its ecosystem and breathe the poisonous air it produces daily. We believe that our feet wander aimlessly on a planet that wanders aimlessly. Without telos, we succumb to emptiness.

Our ancestors, however, had a different story. They believed they lived in a world filled with telos. They believed in meaning and purpose, and they believed it came from above. More than just believing this story, they also crafted ways in which they would regularly and habitually embody and participate in that story. Things that might seem boring or inconsequential to modern people were seen as life-giving, spirit-renewing, and soul-orienting practices. In other words, they not only believed something above existed; they acted it out.

The messaging of our current culture has convinced so many of us that we live in a godless, fatherless, and purposeless story. Materialism says there is no God, life is a product of chance, and if our lives do have any purpose, it's merely what we humans invent and ascribe to it. As we wonder, *Does my life matter in any real sense? Does my life have any real meaning? Is there someone above who even cares?* materialism answers with an emphatic "No!" Materialism robs us of the things humans have always held firmly. Humans were never meant to live in this environment. This environment is making us sick. We can't live a meaningful life under these conditions. What is a life without telos? What a sad story we have inherited! The good news is this is not the only story. There is an alternative story that you not only believe in, but participate in.

To find our way out of the materialist story, we are going to have to journey back in time and discover some old words, tools, and wisdom that will help us better understand how we got here and how we can get out. Consider the following a road map for this book: In part one we will explore the causes and symptoms of our current condition: what happened, why we feel empty, and the effects of materialism on our lives. In part two we will look to the past to find the remedy in the ancient wisdom of our ancestors, specifically the practices they used to properly orient themselves in the world and cultivate a meaningful life. These practices give answers to life's most important questions and give us a different story to live in. Think of it as the medicine we need to combat the effects of materialism and ultimately get rid of the sickness. We will spend most of our time in this section. Part three closes the book by looking at the mechanics of how these remedies not only combat materialism but ultimately shape us into the people we were designed to be.

When modern life is *empty*, know there is a path toward *fullness*. Life is filled with meaning and purpose. The truth, goodness, and beauty that you long for has a source, but materialism has blinded us to it. The good news is that the Christian faith has the tools to give sight to the blind. Let's begin this journey by returning to our first and foundational word from the past: telos.

PREGNANT WITH TELOS

After my wife and I had our first child, it was not long before we started talking about having a second. Now, you would think that after the pain of our first child, my wife might respond with, "Are you kidding me? Do you know how horrible that was?" Which is totally understandable. Having a human being growing inside of you and then coming out of your body is not a walk in the park. There is significant pain, danger, and anxiety that come with pregnancy.

Nevertheless, she wanted to have another baby. And my wife is not some weird statistical anomaly that somehow, despite the pain, wanted to have another child. It's actually common for women to say, "Let's have another." So, what in the world could possibly make a sane woman sign up for that nine-month ordeal again? The answer is telos. There is a point and purpose to pregnancy. And the love, beauty, and glory that comes as a result makes it all worth it. Pain is worth enduring if there is a purpose.

Think about some of the hard stuff you have done in life. Did those events not have some type of end goal? Some aim or purpose? Why does a professional athlete train so hard? Is it not to win the championship? Why does a college student study so rigorously? Is it not to pass the test and graduate?

You endure pain and difficulty for a greater good.

What happens to us when we endure the pain of life, but there is no telos on the other end? No victory, no championship, no graduation? The pain loses its purpose. It becomes meaningless pain. And to endure meaningless pain is unbearable.

You can have a smaller-sized telos to fuel smaller endeavors. Getting a college degree can motivate you to put up with classes you don't like. Working extra hard and long hours with the hope of a promotion can propel you forward. Getting up early before work to jog is inspired by the goal of running a marathon. The harder the task, however, the greater the telos needed. Planning on going through labor? Better be something wonderfully amazing like a baby on the other side.

But what about life itself? What can motivate you to endure the pain of life? Sure, sometimes life is easy, but sometimes life hits you like a freight train. It hits you harder than you ever thought you could be hit. What do you do when it seems like there is nothing in the world that could enable you to endure?

How does the modern world deal with this type of pain? What purpose can be given to suffering in the materialist story? Fredrich Nietzsche, himself an atheist, once said, "He who has a why to live for can bear almost any how."[5] Without a great "why" to live, things that were once bearable for previous generations become unbearable for us.

Author and psychologist Viktor Frankl, who endured the horror of the Holocaust and lost his wife to the Nazis, expanded on this. In his time in the concentration camps, he encouraged fellow prisoners on the brink of despair. He wrote, "Whenever there was an opportunity for it, one had to give them a why—an aim—for their lives, in order to strengthen them to bear the terrible *how* of their existence. Woe to him who saw no more sense in his life, no aim, no purpose, and therefore no point in carrying on. He was soon lost."[6]

When you read the history of what people endured when they had telos, it's remarkable.

People overcame hell. Everyday life for many was filled with immense suffering and pain. For example, child mortality rates until recent human history were horrendous. An incredible percentage of families had to endure the loss of a child. In ancient Rome, many children were not named in their first week of life due to death being such a high probability.[7] On top of that, there was always the great existential fear of raiding forces, famine, drought, or plague that were very real threats. Nevertheless, people endured, they lived life, and they could speak of joy.

In the Westminster Shorter Catechism, a question is asked: "What is the chief end of man?" The answer given: "Man's chief end is to glorify God, and to enjoy him forever."[8] We might say a "chief end" is similar to something like an ultimate telos, a telos that is of highest importance.

Various religions have similar statements and beliefs. And although I contend that Christianity is uniquely true, the point is that no matter what your religious background was, for thousands of years people's lives had a higher purpose: to serve that which was above. It was what was above that gave you meaning below. It was what existed up there that gave your feet down here something to stand on.

A helpful word for "that which is above" is *transcendence*. Transcendent things are above or beyond the material world. From the transcendent world our ancestors derived meaning and purpose.

But an important question has stared down at the modern individual. What if there is nothing above? What if we truly wander aimlessly down here below? What if meaning and purpose are just the creation of clever humans trying to convince themselves this life is actually worth living? What if we are, in fact, all alone?

The good news is that there is nothing new under the sun. People have wrestled with these issues for a long time. We are not the first to look up at the sun and ask, "Is there anything above?" And even though the modern world has answered that question with a resounding "No!" our ancestors wrestled with that same question and came to a different conclusion. And for that we turn to a very old book titled Qoheleth.

3

Hevel

HUNDREDS OF YEARS BEFORE THE TIME OF JESUS, there was an ancient book of wisdom in Hebrew titled *Qoheleth*. Most people who are familiar with the book today know it by a translation of its Greek name, Ecclesiastes. *Qoheleth*, however, is a Hebrew word that means something like "someone who gathers an assembly of people together to give instruction or direction." In other words, a teacher or preacher of some sort. In this ancient book, Qoheleth the teacher ponders the problem of meaninglessness. He looks at the entirety of our world and at the lives we've lived under the sun and declares:

> Vanity of vanities! All is vanity.
> What does man gain by all the toil
>   at which he toils under the sun? (Ecclesiastes 1:2-3)

This word *vanity* becomes a theme that is repeated forty times throughout the book's twelve chapters. In the book's context, the word *vanity* does not mean an abundance of pride in oneself but rather the quality of being empty or worthless. This is why some Bible translations use the word *meaningless* rather than *vanity*. Qoheleth examines every domain of reality and with shocking pessimism states, again and again, that all is vanity. To be precise, he states that everything *under the sun* is vanity. Everything we do down here on this planet is vanity. Our work, our loves, our achievements . . . all vanity. Does this sound familiar? Without some telos from above that is bigger and grander than the harshness of life, the bleakness of reality sets in.

But it gets even worse. The Hebrew word that is translated "vanity" has a much deeper, profound, and disturbing meaning. This is not to say that "vanity" is a bad translation. The problem is that our English word *vanity* is too small of a word to carry the large cargo that the Hebrew word does. The Hebrew word is *hevel*, and hevel has layers of meaning in the biblical world. At its most basic level, hevel simply means "vapor." But vapor as an image communicates much more. A vapor is something that is here for a brief moment and then gone. Now think about that for a second. How much of life is *here today and gone tomorrow*?

Think of a sunset at the end of a beautiful day. Now imagine a newly-fallen-in-love couple sitting there on a blanket, taking it in. Both of them are looking at the sun setting and are in awe of its beauty. They are both silent because deep down they know this moment is about to flee. They wish this moment could last longer as they grasp each other's hands, but it won't . . . and it never will. Suns always set. Before you can take in all of the sun's beauty, it sinks below the horizon and is gone. Beautiful sunsets are hevel. They are that which is here for a moment and gone the next. How many of life's most beautiful experiences are hevel?

Do you remember cold days as a child? Remember when you would exhale and marvel that your breath was somehow making magic clouds appear? Remember how, as a child, you would sometimes try to reach up and grab your breath? But as your hand grasped at the little, personal magic cloud you had just created, it was gone. Your breath on a cold day is hevel: here for a moment and gone the next.[1]

Another aspect of hevel is the fact that vapor is formless. Many ancient people would look at things like vapor, smoke, or lifting fog as something without solid shape. The structure of something that is hevel is unstable. Think of blowing in the direction of smoke. The smoke simply moves with the air and disappears. It is partially due to an unstable structure that something is here for a moment and gone the next. The structure has no lasting power.

Is your life an unstable structure that is here today and gone tomorrow?

Perhaps the most haunting way to illustrate hevel is found in the story of Cain and Abel. The account appears within the first few pages of the Bible. This story, like the rest found in Genesis, is formative. Genesis sets in motion everything that comes after. In other words, these stories are those through which we are to see the rest of the stories of Scripture.

Immediately after the first humans are exiled from their garden paradise, they have their first children. The oldest is named Cain and the younger Abel. The story does not give us the precise details as to why, but Cain's offering is rejected while Abel's is accepted by God. Cain becomes enraged because of this. The short story ends with Cain murdering his brother. The story is brutal but is even more haunting when we realize the name given to Eve's son. The Hebrew word that Eve gave Abel as a name was *Hevel*. That's right, the same word Qoheleth uses. Eve's son is, by name, that which is here today and gone tomorrow. He is a vapor before her eyes.

What makes all of this even more depressing is this predicament scales to all of us. Hevel is the fate of all humans. We are all Abel. We are all here today and gone tomorrow.

DUST TO DUST

In the Bible, the first human created is named Adam. And in Hebrew his name is . . . wait for it . . . *Adam*. But *Adam* in Hebrew is not just a name; it literally means "man." So, the first man is named *man*, or in Hebrew, the first Adam is named *Adam*.

Additionally, this first Adam/man is made from the dust of the earth: "Then the LORD God formed the man of dust from the ground and breathed into his nostrils the breath of life, and the man became a living creature" (Genesis 2:7).

The Hebrew is interesting at this point because the Hebrew word for ground is *adamah*. Adam is made from adamah. Adam is a creature of dirt made from the ground; he is of the earth. The reason this is so poignant is because the first human life begins from the ground, and ultimately human life ends in the ground. God says to the creature of dirt:

> By the sweat of your face
>   you shall eat bread,
> till you return to the ground,
>   for out of it you were taken;
> for you are dust,
>   and to dust you shall return. (Genesis 3:19)

Adam is destined to return to the adamah. All humans are children of death, destined to return to the dust we came from. It is the inescapable reality looming over humanity; the shadow of death is ever on us.

I have officiated many funerals and one constant theme is loved ones always wanting more time. This is certainly true in tragic deaths, when someone loses someone far too young. But the sentiment still appears with people who, by all relevant standards, lived a long and happy life. Their loved ones still say things like, "I wish I had a little more time with them," or "I wish I could have one more day."

Life is always hevel.

There is an unavoidable reality to all of this. No matter who you are or what you have done, death will come for you. And consider this potentially depressing fact, even the most remarkable people who live the most remarkable lives are forgotten within a few generations of their life. Try naming the tenth president of the United States. Did you guess John Tyler? How about the eleventh, or twelfth? Can you name the thirteenth president? How could you forget about our great thirteenth president of the United States, Millard Fillmore? Don't tell me you forgot about Millard!

Sure, there are some exceptions, but they are certainly exceptions. Most people know George Washington and Abraham Lincoln, but even then, unless you are a historian who studies their lives, you know very little about them. Who were their kids? What were their hobbies? Do you personally care about these former presidents in any real, meaningful way?

For the most part, even if you become the president of the United States of America, within a few generations no one will remember you and no one will care. Within two generations there is a good chance your great-grandchildren will not even know your name. Bleak, right?

Hevel. Everything is hevel.

FRUIT FLIES AND TADPOLES

My kids and I once saved some tadpoles from dying in a puddle that was about to dry up. The kids could see the puddle was very small and could not bear to leave the tadpoles to die under the heat of the sun. So, we did some quick research and created a new puddle with the necessary environmental features for them to continue to grow. As they grew into frogs, we needed a good food supply. The local pet store had the solution: in small tubes about three inches long with the circumference of a quarter, you could take home about twenty fruit flies.

Fruit flies are extremely small but make a delicious meal for baby frogs. Now this is where it gets crazy. You can almost guarantee that upon purchase, these fruit flies have already laid eggs in the tube. They are likely too small for anyone to notice, but they are there.

How can one be so sure? Well, fruit flies go from being an egg to adulthood in a little more than a week. And once they reach adulthood, they will usually begin mating within a few hours.

This process commences with the male initiating a courtship ritual where he shows off his special moves. He will dance around the female and move his wings at certain speeds to create vibrations that function as a sort of "lets-hook-up-girl" jingle.[2] Who knew fruit flies could be this smooth? Then, in the next twenty-four hours, a new generation of fruit fly eggs will emerge. From egg to adulthood to being new mommy and daddy fruit flies, all of this happens in a little more than a week!

When pet stores sell these fruit fly tubes, they place a good food source for the flies at the bottom of the tube, which means you get a little closed-system fruit fly world. Within a few weeks you can watch several generations of fruit flies live and die (through the admirable death of being eaten by baby frogs).

Fruit flies and their children's children live their entire lives before us in several weeks. They live, die, and then are forgotten.

Are we like fruit flies? Small, insignificant creatures living a pointless life in a test tube, destined to die after living a brief, meaningless existence? Do we live in a closed system with nothing above? As people of dust, are we destined to live and die and be forgotten like fruit flies? Sounds like hevel, right? See how the words of Qoheleth capture this:

> There is no remembrance of former things,
>   nor will there be any remembrance
> of later things yet to be
>   among those who come after. (Ecclesiastes 1:11)

Is there a part of you that gets it? Is there a part of you that's nodding your head with Qoheleth, saying, "Yep, that is how it is." You work your whole life and then die. Dust to dust. When you look at the world, you can perfectly identify with Qoheleth. It's like there is a time machine, and a three-thousand-year-old document is proclaiming the thoughts and beliefs of the despair of modern materialism.[3]

> For what happens to the children of man and what happens to the beasts is the same; as one dies, so dies the other. They all have the same breath, and man has no advantage over the beasts, for all is vanity. All go to one place. All are from the dust, and to dust all return. (Ecclesiastes 3:19-20)

Does that not sound like it would fit in the modern world's meaningless landscape? What about this:

> I saw all the oppressions that are done under the sun. And behold, the tears of the oppressed, and they had no one to comfort them! On the side of their oppressors there was power, and there was no one to comfort them. And I thought the dead who are already dead more fortunate than the living who are still alive. But better than both is he who has not yet been and has not seen the evil deeds that are done under the sun. (Ecclesiastes 4:1-3)

Does this not resonate with the attitudes of so many in our present time? Let's look at one last insight from Qoheleth. He poetically proclaims:

> Time is a valuable thing
> Watch it fly by as the pendulum swings. . . .
> I tried so hard, And got so far
> But in the end, it doesn't even matter.[4]

Okay, Qoheleth didn't say that. That was Linkin Park's song "In the End." But there is a reason why that song resonated so profoundly with the culture. Its lyrics are in the air we breathe. In the materialist understanding of life, it all ends the same.

At this point you might be wondering, *How in the world is this book* Qoheleth *in the Bible?* I mean, when people think of the Bible, they think mostly of a book of hope, encouragement, and the promise of a life after this one. So far, however, it seems like this book is merely preaching the emptiness of materialism.

A NEEDED TURN

As an ancient book, Qoheleth could easily be disregarded as irrelevant for the modern world, but that move would be foolish. If there was a book for our time, it is this one. Although written roughly three thousand years ago, Qoheleth reads like a modern materialist handbook. There is nothing above, no one coming to save, nothing worth striving for. Nothing to make the suffering of life worth it. Of course, all of this is true if there is nothing above the sun.

However, the book makes a turn that nearly all ancient people made—a turn that has been abandoned by materialism but is desperately needed in our modern world. After giving hints along the way that there might be more to the story, near the end of the book the author concludes by saying all of this pessimism is true under the sun. But then Qoheleth pivots and seems to say there actually is something above the sun. As a reader you are like, "Wait, what? Is there a point to life after all?" Qoheleth concludes by speaking of things above the sun, and don't think Qoheleth is thinking about things above the sun in the sense of objects in outer space. Ancient people were not stupid. They were not talking about the sun in a strictly materialist sense. They were speaking of heavenly realities, and by heavenly reality I do not merely mean the place you get to go to when you die. I am speaking of ultimate reality—a reality so real that it grounds ours. If that world does not exist, then indeed our world is just a floating rock in space so grand it would not even receive honorable mention in a list of the top one billion largest floating rocks.

But what if there is something above the sun? What if there is something that transcends us? It's above us in one sense but below us in the sense that it is the foundation on which our world is built. If there is something above the sun, it is from that reality that we must find ultimate meaning.

We must look up. If we are going to find any stable structure, anything that is more than hevel, anything that can ground us in this ever-changing world, we must find something that is unchanging and eternal.

If we keep our eyes only on that which is below the sun, then we will ultimately become a below-the-sun type of people. But we were made for more, we long for more, we thirst for meaning.

Like us, many of our ancestors looked out at the world and wondered, *Is this all there is?* It was not as if modern science and discovery came along and for the first time people began to ask this question. They did, however, make a turn, a turn that we have failed to make.

Ancient people made the decision to look up, and they did so because there were things down here that tilted their gaze upward. They recognized that even things in the material world point to another world. If there is something that transcends us, then we ought to see something like expressions of that reality down here. To understand this, we need to turn to more old words.

4

Truth, Goodness, Beauty

FROM ANCIENT GREEK MINDS like Plato to medieval thinkers like Aquinas, many of history's greatest philosophers have spoken of transcendentals. Transcendentals are universal properties in all beings. There is a long debate about how many transcendentals there are and exactly how we ought to go about defining them, but for much of the philosophical tradition of the West they were accepted and expounded on. I know all this talk of "properties of being" might sound incredibly technical, but the transcendentals are actually quite easy to understand when we approach them not in the abstract but from our own human experience.

The Christian tradition has said that every human being has a longing for truth, goodness, and beauty. Three transcendentals we can experience here below that come from above. Ultimately, these transcendentals find their source in the being of God.

Think of it like this: we can apprehend the transcendent God above, in three domains. Each domain has a corresponding transcendental:

We apprehend God in the domain of reason (truth).

We apprehend God in the domain of morality (goodness).

We apprehend God in the domain of aesthetics (beauty).

Truth, goodness, and beauty come from above; they are cosmic values. Humans are made in such a way that we are wired to experience and long for these values from above, here down below.

Have you ever been bothered by the feeling that the news is not telling you the truth? Ever been lied to? Ever wished that those in authority would just tell the truth?

Have you ever been wronged and felt the anger of mistreatment? Been cut off on the freeway? Heard of something so horrific that your innermost being cried out for justice?

Have you ever heard a song that did something to you deep down? That moved you in a way that mere song should not be able to do? And then when it was over, you immediately wanted to hear it again?

We all have these experiences. Transcendentals can be hard to explain, but we know them when we encounter them. We want to know the truth, see wrongs righted, and behold the beautiful.

Who wants to live in an untrue, unjust, ugly world?

LEARNING TO LOOK UP

Picture yourself on a white-sand beach with that ever-fleeting sunset we talked about earlier. You behold the beauty and you want it to last, but just as you are attempting to take it all in, the sun drops below the horizon. Your horizontal gaze can no longer see the beauty. In one sense, that experience is over, but what the transcendentals do—when rightly observed—is encourage us to look up to their source. In other words, you can behold an object and experience its truth, goodness, or beauty and let that be the end of it. Or you can follow the path the object is leading you on.

At first, we see something beautiful in the horizontal, but the question remains: Where does the beauty come from? To this question, the Christian story has an answer. A first-century follower of Jesus states, "Every good gift and every perfect gift is from above, coming down from the Father of lights, with whom there is no variation or shadow due to change" (James 1:17).

Notice the language—it's important. God himself is the source of every good gift. The being of God is the location from which all goodness comes. It is from above but received below. This source is also unchanging, a characteristic that theologians refer to as the immutability of God. His being has no shadow. He is pure radiance, and his goodness never changes. There are no corners of darkness hidden away in him.

James is saying that everything we experience down here, if it is good, true, or beautiful, ultimately is a gift of God and comes from above. These gifts received find their source in his very being. In other words, when we experience the true, the good, and the beautiful down here in the horizontal, we should immediately tilt our heads and *look up*. It's as if the transcendentals have lines coming out of them that point us upward, directing us to set our gaze on the vertical reality they lead to. A Christian doxology captures this sentiment well when it says, "Praise God from whom all blessings flow, Praise him all creatures here below."

But what happens when a culture loses the concept of anything transcendent above? Truth, goodness, and beauty become ends in themselves; they don't lead anywhere, and they never make you look up. Truth, goodness, and beauty become hevel. Sure, they might be good in the moment, but like smoke, they have no stability in their structure.

Why pursue the highest of truth, the highest of goodness, the highest of beauty? Truth, goodness, and beauty become valuable only in what they can do for us in the temporary. We pursue them as long as they serve us, but we never follow their upward lead. We love *love*, never asking, "Where did this gift come from?"

What happens when the reporters, the artists, the scientists, or the everyday person on the street no longer see truth, goodness, and beauty as things with cosmic value? Is there a difference between an architect who designs a building for a customer who is focused only on the cost and function of the building, and an architect who believes he is designing a cathedral for the glory of God? Is there a difference between a reporter who believes truth is grounded in a being who will divide all truth from falsehood, and one who thinks truth is merely one's personal opinion? Is there a difference between someone who believes "greater love has no one than this, that someone lay down his life for his friends" (John 15:13), and someone who believes human life has no value worthy of sacrifice?

The abandonment of the transcendentals is the natural next step for a culture who denies their source. And this has real, concrete implications for any culture that makes this move. We abandon the transcendentals, and the One to whom they point, at our own peril.

Does any of this feel familiar, as if it is taking place right before our eyes?

Does it feel like there is a lot less truth, goodness, and beauty in our culture today? Does it feel like we are not only *not* committed to the good, the true, and the beautiful but have gone even further? Does it feel as though, at least at some level, our culture has adopted a commitment to something like the anti-transcendentals: the false, the evil, and the ugly?

LEFTOVERS

At this point you might be saying, "Wait a second, I know plenty of people who still pursue the good, the true, and the beautiful without a belief in God—people who believe and live as if the true, the good, and the beautiful matter. They live as if there really is a supreme good for their life." It's true, of course, that people who don't believe in God can do so. However, the real question is, How long can one consistently pursue these things while maintaining they are without any transcendent grounding?

A culture like ours can live off the religious leftovers of Christianity, but those leftovers won't last forever. This can be seen time and time again at funerals. I have heard atheists at funerals say something like, "We know that Grandma is in a better place." Wait, what? Grandma is in a better place? In cases like this there is a holding on to some of the leftovers from the meal that Christianity provided. Many are eager to eat the leftovers while denying the hands that prepared the food to begin with. The meal was great, and the leftovers still taste incredible, but eventually the leftovers will run out. A consistent denial of God will saturate all levels of belief. In many cases today the pure, undiluted nihilism has not yet fully set in. But it will.

Or you might hear a materialist speak of human rights. But where do these rights come from? Universal human rights were not assumed by ancient people. The average modern person might affirm them but is completely unaware that it's only because of two thousand years of Christian tradition that they even believe in them. If human beings are mere physical matter, where are their rights located? Can you point to them? Where do they come from?

The leftovers of Christianity are so good that in our culture you might see someone criticize the church for its treatment of women, the poor, the vulnerable, or some other group, all the while not even recognizing that the very ruler and metric they are using to critique the church is the metric given to them by the church.

Where do we suppose the idea came from that all people have intrinsic and innate value? History demonstrates this was not the default position of humanity. Universal human rights flowed from the idea that all people are made in the image of God. Materialism loves to eat the fruit of Christianity while not acknowledging the tree that grew it.

These are but a couple of examples of how people can live and think inconsistently, holding on to the hopes and values that the Christian faith gave while simultaneously abandoning it. Without the proper foundation, you can try and build meaning, purpose, morality, and telos, but eventually the structure will collapse.

One can try and find meaning in lesser things, of course. It's easy to find meaning in family, romance, love, children, or career. But why do those things matter? If love matters, why does it matter? If having a solid work ethic is a good thing, why is it good? If treating your family poorly is wrong, why is it wrong? Is there something, someone, or some authority above us?

The question takes us back to Qoheleth.

Qoheleth answers the question with an astounding "Yes!" There is something above us. And we ought to live as if every moment matters, because it does matter. There is One who sees all and knows all, and it's not only to dust that we will return; we will return to *him*.

As Qoheleth says, "The end of the matter; all has been heard. Fear God and keep his commandments, for this is the whole duty of man. For God will bring every deed into judgment, with every secret thing, whether good or evil" (Ecclesiastes 12:13-14).

In other words, for the modern person, the book of Qoheleth is like a thought experiment on the philosophy of materialism. If the material world is all that exists, then everything here is hevel. It's meaningless. Its vanity. What's fascinating is that this thought experiment was not done by a modern nihilistic materialist, it was done by a man living millennia ago who was wrestling with the same problems we still have today.

Qoheleth looks at every layer and domain of reality and sees how very easy it is to say, "Hevel, all is hevel." He ends, however, by looking upward. He looks beyond our mere material existence and says, "There is someone above, and it is in him you find your purpose."

Without this, life is truly hevel.

You might be able to borrow meaning and purpose from religion, but eventually you will have to give it back. You will need something above and beyond your mere material existence to ground yourself. The leftovers will run out; you will need to return to their source.

When you stop believing there is something transcendent above, you stop looking up. And when a culture, people, or individual stops looking up, the consequences are severe. When we stop looking up, we become horizontal creatures. Horizontal humans.

Humanity was not made to set their gaze on the mere horizontal. We were made to look up. Humans were not made to be animals. We were not made to crawl. We were made to stand up. We were made to be vertical creatures with our heads tilted to the heavens.

Human bodies are like trees pushing toward the sky. As trees reach for the sun, we, too, reach for the good, the true, and the beautiful. We are meant to reach for the One from whom all blessings flow.

But when trees do not get enough sun, they cease growing, they become weak, they shrink, and they die. A horizontal humanity is destined for the same end.

What are the symptoms of a horizontal humanity? What are the symptoms of a people that are sick and malnourished? What happens when we believe the materialist story and cease looking up, thus keeping our eyes fixed on the horizontal? There are many signs and symptoms of a horizontal humanity, but at least in our culture, the phenomena can be observed occurring in two opposite extremes.

Humans are meant to grow into healthy and mature adults, but a horizontal human will be pulled away from their proper center. If they get pulled in one direction, they will become infantile; if they get pulled in the opposite direction, they will turn into something approximating death. Horizontal humans morph into either toddlers or zombies.

That may sound strange, but over the next couple of chapters we will look closely at what I mean and examine both of these extremes.

5

Toddlers

WHEN MY DAUGHTER WAS A TODDLER, she loved a particular blanket. And when I say she loved this blanket, I mean she *loved* this blanket. It was nothing great to behold. It was not even really a blanket to begin with. It was more like a two-foot-square piece of fabric that was used as a blanket. Its color can best be described as somewhere between purple and pink. To the normal eye, this was just a small piece of fabric, but to my two-year-old, this was the great and mighty and awesome and powerful "little blankie"!

At first, the blanket did not have these attributes. It was just something she held one night that helped her fall asleep as she squeezed it between her arms. But over the course of the following weeks, this falling asleep with little blankie happened a few more times, and soon she was asking for it every night. Little blankie became essential in the nighttime ritual of "going nigh nigh." It became a necessary comfort for her.

If you tried to take her little blankie, you would get "the look," a look that is surprising from a toddler. It was a look that said, "Don't you even dare think about taking little blankie. It will only end in regret, Mom and Dad."

Little blankie was soon held throughout the day as well. She would set it aside to perform a task, but she would know exactly where she put it down and go back for it when the task was finished.

Little blankie was close by at breakfast. And at lunch. And at dinner. If she fell and got hurt, as toddlers often do as they master their sprinting skills, the tears would start to roll and the call would begin: "I need Mommy, and I need little blankie!" Little blankie became central to everything. You took it away at your own peril. In her toddler mind, having little blankie was a life-and-death issue.

What exactly is taking place in this strange relationship between toddler and blanket? The toddler, in a sense, is unknowingly assigning religious significance to the blanket. The blanket becomes a comfort and presence needed to face the world. Without the blanket the world is too much. The night is too scary, the fall too hard, the vegetables too gross. But with the power of little blankie, the child can courageously face the day.

Now anyone who has raised a child knows that this occurs with all sorts of things: a blanket, a doll, a stuffed animal, a toy truck. Kids assign a great deal of value to objects that really are not meant to carry such weight. These objects work great in helping toddlers react to the lights going out at bedtime, a hard fall, or having to eat vegetables, but they were never meant to carry the weight of life's biggest problems.

Nevertheless, we don't fault toddlers for assigning such significance to insignificant things. It's a part of their development. But eventually, little blankie must go. Children can't continue to rely on these things for security and safety. Many parents remember the day when they helped their child move beyond the need for such objects, and for the most part they remember many tears being shed that day.

Part of the job of parents is helping their children see the type of meaning and value they are attributing to their favorite objects and then helping them adjust appropriately. If parents do not do this, they stunt the growth of their child. They leave them in a toddler-like state, a state that assigns too great a meaning to lesser things. And here is the massive problem with that: lesser things cannot bear the weight assigned to them. Little blankie cannot bear the weight of the world. It can when the weight of the world is as simple as eating your vegetables or going to sleep, but it cannot when it comes to the real pains of life.

The pains, problems, and suffering of life can be immense. For such heavy matters you must have something strong enough to carry them. Only the transcendent can truly carry the weight of existential matters. Better put, only things above can bear the full weight of things below.

So, what happens when an entire culture refuses to mature and begins to assign ultimate meaning and purpose to lesser things? What happens when the tenets of materialism rule the day? What happens when God is removed, religion is sidelined, and the transcendentals are forgotten? What happens when we fail to look up for the meaning that can ground our feet below? Nonreligious objects and activities begin to function like religion.

A MODERN RITUAL

Every Sunday a ritual takes place that you might be familiar with. It's a ritual that follows a schedule, which follows the placement and movement of the stars. Like all sacred time, there is a rhythm to it.

The ritual takes place in one centralized location. Locals gather at this centralized location, but others also gather in smaller, less organized locations to participate in the ritual. As the ritual proceeds, people raise their hands, shout, and stand on their feet; some are even known to shed tears in the ritual. And in some strange, magical, vicarious transaction, many even find personal victory in the victory achieved by the ritual.

You know what I'm talking about? That's right—football.

You might be saying, "C'mon, I know people love football, but it's not really replacing God or functioning in a religious manner."

Are you sure about that?

Every Sunday there are countless kids who do not dare approach their dad because the team lost. They are familiar with that whisper from their mom, "Don't bother your dad right now; the game just ended." Think about that. How ridiculous is it that a grown man is so emotionally bothered by the outcome of a football game taking place miles away that his own children are fearful to even approach him?

Or go in the opposite direction: let's say the team wins. You might hear someone say, "Aw man, I have to go back to work tomorrow. But at least the team won, so I'm starting the week on a good note." The whole tone of the upcoming week is influenced by the outcome of the game!

There is a reason we often perform this ritual on Sunday.

THE GLUE THAT HOLDS THINGS TOGETHER

I grew up watching the Los Angeles Lakers. After the tragic passing of the legendary basketball player Kobe Bryant, I saw an interview with musician and actor Ice Cube discussing the monumental loss that it was to the people of Southern California.[1] Without fully realizing it at the time, what I heard Ice Cube articulate were some of the most profound insights into the religious nature of the athlete.

The host began the interview by saying that when people thought of Los Angeles, they thought of the Hollywood sign and Kobe Bryant. She then asked Ice Cube, "What did he mean to the people here?" His response:

> You know, people don't understand how much an athlete like Kobe or Kareem or Shaq or Magic, how much they really hold this city together. You know, the city has a lot of fault lines, not only in the ground but with the people. And what brings us together is the love for our teams. . . . It gives us something, you know, to unite behind, [because in LA we have] gang banging, economic differences, racial differences, and our teams hold us together. So, you know, Kobe is some of the glue that holds LA together.

This is profound. If you are unfamiliar with Southern California, he is saying that not only do they have literal fault lines that cause literal catastrophes, but they also have social and cultural fault lines: gang violence, economic struggles, racial tensions, and more. And then he gets to something incredibly revealing: Kobe was part of the glue that held it all together.

And he is right. If you watched a Lakers game in person, it might be the only time you saw that diverse of a group gathering around the same cause. In the Kobe era, Lakers games created a unity around something greater than individual differences. Rich, poor, White, Black, Hispanic, Asian, this gang, that gang . . . everyone put those differences aside for a few hours and chanted, "Kobe! Kobe! Kobe!"

When the game is on, there is a unity of purpose and vision. The court is sacred space, and game time is sacred time. There is a battle taking place on that floor. You have a champion who fights the battle for you. He has fought many battles before. You have seen him deliver you on the court many times before. He fights for you. He fights for LA.

In ancient times, religion was the glue that held people together. It was what brought a society together and shaped the culture. Without that, what brings the people together? In today's world, what can make people put differences aside and unite on something greater than themselves? It's no longer Zeus, Athena, or Ares; it's Lebron James, Travis Kelce, Lionel Messi, or fill in the blank.

To be clear, there is nothing wrong with giving value to sports. The issue is this: To what degree does one value sports? When a sport, a team, or an athlete becomes one of our top priorities in life—in other words, when sports begin to function like religion—that's where the problem lies. When we say things like, "I bleed purple and gold" (the Lakers' team colors) or "Lakers are life in this house"; when other events are canceled because nothing can compete with "game time"; when children are afraid to approach their father because his team lost; that's when we know we aren't dealing with sports anymore. We are dealing with religion. Keep in mind that people have been murdered for cheering for the wrong team in the wrong location.[2]

But this type of religion always fails because the inevitable always happens: the game ends. Sometimes the team wins and sometimes they lose, but one way or another the game ends. No matter what happens, a team cannot carry the weight of life's biggest problems. The anticipation of the Friday night game might help you slug through a hard day at the end of the workweek, but it won't sustain you when life hits you like a freight train. After all, it's just a highly developed and more advanced form of a little blankie.

Remember, a little blanket is not bad in and of itself. Blankets can and should give comfort to little kids, but kids must become adults and realize that blankets are not sufficient for giving life the structural stability necessary to deal with the realities of existence. Likewise, sports are fun and appropriate, but don't think for a moment that they can carry you through this life in any meaningful manner.

Basketball won't save you when the doctor gives you bad news. An athlete will not bring comfort when your marriage is falling apart. When you are on your deathbed, you won't be saying, "I wish I could have watched one more game." And if you do, what a sad state to find yourself in. You will be dying as a toddler, not as a mature adult.

As a pastor, I have seen when someone is on their deathbed and they look back on their life and on all the emptiness they pursued. I have seen the loved ones come in to say their goodbyes. I have talked with them as they shared how much they loved their father, but how hard it was to live with him and how broken their relationship is now. I have heard the future widow say, "Not much will change. He never paid all that much attention to me." But I have seen the light bulb click on when the one who is dying gets it. They finally see it. They realize how much they wasted, how what they thought was important did not matter very much when death was at their door. You haven't seen guilt and regret until you've seen it at the end.

And here is the scary part: in the blink of an eye, you will be there. You will be at the end of your own life. What will you look back on? A life that pursued the highest of truth, goodness, and beauty, or a life that pursued hevel? Materialism keeps your eyes focused on the horizontal, on the things below. A life of meaning is a life with eyes focused upward.

Human beings are constantly assigning religious value to things that are not worthy of the assignment, and this phenomenon is observed in every area of our culture. When a culture loses God above, it will inevitably begin making little blankies out of anything and everything.

Go online and find a forum where people are discussing comic books. Try and find a thread titled something like "Marvel vs. DC." Grab some popcorn and begin to scroll. You will very quickly see people losing their minds arguing about which one is better. Whole essays are written. You would think this was a debate on Christianity versus Islam. You would think people were debating life-and-death issues, things of utmost importance. You would think they were talking about which God is the true God.

Well, maybe it is something like that.

Ever hear of a Swiftie (a devoted fan of Taylor Swift)? Ever met someone who is such a Swiftie that it has become a foundational pillar of their identity? Ever seen a grown man scream at the top of his lungs watching WWE (dramatized and scripted wrestling) as if evil were truly about to defeat good? Ever seen someone care more about what is taking place in a video game world than what is taking place in the real world?

We no longer have Greek gods and goddesses . . . we have Taylor Swift, and politics, and video games, and comic books, and . . . the list goes on. We are little blankie-making machines. Do you see it out there? Do you see it in yourself?

RIGHT ORDERING

This is not to look down on all of the things we humans find entertaining and pleasurable. It is not as if all of these things are inherently wrong. Remember, it is not the object or the activity itself that is the issue, it's the ordering.

For example, someone might say that they live for God, family, country, and the Lakers—and then add, "And in that order." Immediately, a relative responds by saying, "Yeah right, more like Lakers, God, family, country!" Still another relative chimes in with something like, "He puts the team before God." Now, we know what the family is trying to say, but their language is not accurate. When you put something above God, you are not putting something *above* God. Because whatever sits at the top of your hierarchy of values is, by definition, your *God*. So, the Lakers are God. The girlfriend is God. The video game is God. You can't put something above God without making it functionally God.

Whatever the object is, if it sits at the top, all the things below must pay homage to it. The voice from the past says, "You shall have no other gods before me," and for good reason.

Here is the problem: horizontal humans do not reach high enough. They put the weight of life on things that cannot possibly carry the burden. The vehicles they choose are not strong enough to pull the weight. The things they choose are fragile and weak, and they break. Earthly things do not provide heavenly meaning. The things of this earth are always temporary. They will always come crashing down, and entropy will always win.

In 2008 one of these crashes happened. A global economic crisis began. We saw in real time what happens when the gods of a people break under the weight of the pressure put on them. When the money was lost, in many instances the reason for life was lost as well. Pastor and author Tim Keller recalls:

The acting chief financial officer of Freddie Mac, the Federal Home Loan Mortgage Corporation, hanged himself in his basement. The chief executive of Sheldon Good, a leading U.S. real estate auction firm, shot himself in the head behind the wheel of his red Jaguar. A French money manager who invested the wealth of many of Europe's royal and leading families, and who had lost $1.4 billion of his clients' money in Bernard Madoff's Ponzi scheme, slit his wrists and died in his Madison Avenue office. A Danish senior executive with HSBC Bank hanged himself in the wardrobe of his £500-a-night suite in Knightsbridge, London. When a Bear Stearns executive learned that he would not be hired by JPMorgan Chase, which had bought his collapsed firm, he took a drug overdose and leapt from the twenty-ninth floor of his office building. A friend said, 'This Bear Stearns thing . . . broke his spirit.' It was grimly reminiscent of the suicides in the wake of the 1929 stock market crash.[3]

Little blankies always fall apart. They are temporary. They will never be eternal. Their structure is always one of instability. You can trust the markets for a time, but they always crash. These types of gods always break.

Horizontal humans never look up for meaning. Their necks lose the muscles needed to pull their heads up. Their gaze is always set on things below. They believe the materialist story; therefore, their gods will be made of wood and stone, and gold and markets, and pixels, and Taylor Swift. There is nothing new under the sun.

But this toddler-like way of living is not the only thing horizontal humans will do to try and deal with life under the sun. There are other ways that we pursue emptiness. Rather than stay in a stage of infantile immaturity, horizontal humans will often move to the opposite end of life, to a place where deadness can take over the living.

6

Zombies

IT SEEMS LIKE EVERY FEW YEARS another huge zombie movie or TV show comes out. Zombies hold an undying fascination for many people in the modern world. Much like our penchant for vampires and werewolves, we can't quite seem to shake our appetite for zombies either. Perhaps what attracts us to zombies is that they are a sort of hybrid creature, life and death brought together in a single person.

I remember as a small child seeing people stumbling forward with arms stretched out, saying, "Brains, brains, brains!" as they attempted to do their best zombie impersonation. As a little kid, it was terrifying for me. Throughout cinematic history, there have been all sorts of zombies. They range from the slow and weak to the fast and aggressive. Sometimes they look like recently deceased humans, but other times they can appear as nothing more than a walking skeleton with only small portions of remaining flesh. Despite their different representations in the cinematic universes they inhabit, they usually have this in common: zombies are living-dead creatures that have an overwhelming and all-consuming appetite for human flesh.

Zombies think of nothing but their next meal. Zombies don't worry about tomorrow, they don't reflect on existential problems, they don't contemplate philosophy or religion. They live for one thing only—their next meal.

Dan O'Bannon, writer and director of *The Return of the Living Dead*, comments that zombies feast on the brains of the living because it makes them feel better by easing their pain.[1] In one of his zombie films, a conversation occurs between a character named Ernie and a zombie securely tied down on a table:

Ernie: You can hear me?
Zombie Woman: Yes.
Ernie: Why do you eat people?
Zombie Woman: Not people. Brains.
Ernie: Brains only?
Zombie Woman: Yes.
Ernie: Why?
Zombie Woman: The PAIN!
Ernie: What about the pain?
Zombie Woman: The pain of being DEAD!
Ernie: It hurts . . . to be dead.
Zombie Woman: I can feel myself rotting.
Ernie: Eating brains . . . How does that make you feel?
Zombie Woman: It makes the pain go away![2]

What an image: humans that are partially dead but still have enough life in them to hunger. *A zombie's whole purpose is looking for their next fix to ease the pain of their own existence.* Does this sound familiar? Have you seen this? Have you sometimes felt like this? Have you ever acted in a similar fashion?

Zombies have a telos that never goes beyond the hope of immediate and instant gratification. The zombie's whole purpose for living is to get the next meal, and as soon as that meal is done, the hunt for the next meal begins. Zombies are humans trapped in a body of death, looking for something with a semblance of life . . . human flesh. The symbolism is potent.

And this is where the fictional zombie becomes all too real. Our modern world has become a world of instant gratification. Citizens of this materialist world often live for the next and immediate hit of pleasure. This pleasure offers a temporary pause to the pain, but it never satisfies.

The pain, and thus the hunger, always returns.

ADDICTIONS

In the United States, over one hundred thousand lives were lost in 2023 due to drug overdoses.[3] One can see this horrible picture in many of the big cities in the United States. Blocks lined with young people barely walking, staggering, one foot in front of the other, heads tilted down, mumbling words, looking for their next moment of use. As I write this, on the front page of a major news outlet there is an article on how the fentanyl crisis is not only affecting major cities but is also hitting rural areas. The text on the image that links to the article says in bold, "Zombies in the Hills."[4] What a sad state we find ourselves in. Human beings have been so changed by addiction that the vocabulary adopted to describe their behavior is that of the undead.

It's easy to look at extreme examples like this with an eye of superiority and judgment, but the truth is, much of America is participating in this zombie-like behavior in one way or another. For example, 46.3 million people aged twelve or older (or 16.5 percent of the population) met the applicable DSM-5 (*Diagnostic and Statistical Manual of Mental Disorders,* fifth edition) criteria for having a substance use disorder.[5] Fifty-seven percent of Americans admit to being addicted to their phone.[6] Our list of addictions includes social media, entertainment, alcohol, pornography, gambling, and many others. We are people of addictions, a society looking for the next easiest thing to get us through the day.

There is a deep dissatisfaction with life. We see no grand purpose for living. So rather than look up and aim high, we horizontal humans look low, our heads tilted down at the phone, the screen, the bottle, the pill, the needle . . . only objects below the sun receive our gaze. Like zombies, we are creatures living for the next meal. Our motivation: anything that will temporarily pause the boredom and pain of life.

The sinister part is that this disease appears to infect nearly everyone. It is not confined to those who we might say have had really hard lives. Many of us now seem to be overwhelmed with the slightest pain. With the loss of higher categories of meaning and purpose, there is nothing that can sustain the individual through even small amounts of discomfort and pain.

A poll conducted by Gallup found that just 38 percent of Americans say they are satisfied in their life.[7] Think about that for a moment . . . these are *Americans* being polled, people who live in a time with such abundance that our ancestors could have never even dreamed of a world like this. Consider this: even during a two-year pandemic, Americans still had food, clean water, and no invading army storming the city gates and killing our people. We might have lacked toilet paper now and then, but we did not starve. Even in our greatest catastrophic events these days, our lives are leaps and bounds ahead of the vast majority of humans who have lived in most times and places. The modern Western world lives in a promised land and does not even know it.

And whenever anything causes even the slightest level of discomfort, we usually have a means to fix it. Is getting out of bed to turn off the lights too much? Don't worry! There is an app for that. Is the toilet seat too cold in the winter? Don't worry! There are warmers set on timers for your cold wake-up. Have the money to eat out but feeling too lazy to get up and go? Have the food delivered to your door. Dirty house? Robots can clean the floor for you. Paradise has overtaken us, and yet many of us are still not happy. Which prompts the question: What happens when you have everything and you are still not satisfied? What do you do then?

Some just try and get through the day so they can head home and play video games. Others just try to make it to the weekend, when they can drink until they pass out on Friday and Saturday and then spend Sunday sobering up enough to start the grind all over again on Monday. Some just try and make it to the next meal to overeat. Whatever it may be, when you don't have anything grand to live for, you'll settle for small things, craving baby hits of dopamine to get you through.

The pursuit of truth, goodness, and beauty is too hard; it's too much work. Instead, we strive for the small and trivial, anything that will give us the instant gratification that we desire. In this, many begin their zombie-like life—a life without discipline, a life without sacrifice for the greater good, a life that is self-centered and focused on immediate reward. It's a horrible way to live. But remember, zombies don't think about things like this, and zombies don't contemplate how horrible it is to be a zombie. Zombies think only about their next meal.

A LIFE WORTH LIVING

Picture yourself in an old zombie movie. You and two friends are doctors working on a cure. One day, you let your guard down and forget to properly lock and secure the entry point to the room you are staying in. In the middle of the night a zombie breaks in, and you and your two friends immediately grab some weapons. But before you can properly kill this undead creature, the zombie bites your dear friend Zach.

At this point everyone knows what's going to happen to Zach. He is going to turn. But since you are doctors working on a cure, you have hope. You immediately tie Zach down, telling him, "It's okay; you're gonna make it." Over the next few days, Zach indeed turns into a zombie as you continue to work on a cure. He is securely fastened to a table and there is no way he can break free. Every minute of every day, Zombie Zach screams, "Feed me! Flesh! Food! Hungry!" Every moment for Zombie Zach is a moment in which he longs to be fed. His most base appetite becomes his all-consuming purpose for living. As the weeks go by, you make progress until you finally believe you did it. A cure! You tested it on some zombie mice, and they came back to their right mind and became normal mice again.

You say a quick prayer, and through a needle you deliver the cure to Zombie Zach. Over the next few minutes, everything about him changes. He cries out less, and he is less aggressive. The shaking and convulsing that once dominated his body begin to ease. You begin to hope. You begin to believe it's working. As you look at your friend, you see his eyes change. If eyes are the windows to the soul, you are for the first time in a long time seeing the soul of your dear friend.

And then a pause . . . no movement, no screaming, no words. Suddenly, Zach smiles. He says, "You did it. You brought me back. You found a cure." Zach begins to cry tears of happiness. You laugh and cry and rejoice as well.

But then, a grimace of pain. And then a contorting of his right leg. And then a scream of agony from Zach. He cries, "It's coming back, I'm turning! I can't go back! I can't go back! Please, help me. Please!" But there is nothing you can do. You weep as your friend begins to turn back into a zombie. And then come normal Zach's final words, the words that are almost predictable in any zombie movie, the words that are uttered immediately before someone turns into the undead: "Please, kill me."

Why is this scene repeated again and again in zombie movies? And why does it seem to work on the viewer time and time again? It's as if it resonates with our culture at some deep level, like we intuitively know that type of life is not worth living. To be a slave to your most basic appetite, to be a slave to the next hit, to be a slave trapped in an unescapable misery is no life at all. At that point, all hope is lost.

I have talked with many people who admit to feeling as if life is pointless. They will be the first to say that they move from small pleasure to small pleasure. Porn, video games, drugs, drinking, TV . . . whatever it may be, these are all activities that keep us going. We seek anything that will distract us from the terrifying truth that maybe, just maybe, there is no point to all of this.

Ever witness a teenager's video game console being taken away? Ever watch a mom try and take her daughter's phone? Ever observe an alcoholic get denied another drink? The reactions are very similar. It's as if the person's life itself is being threatened.

This zombie-like sickness is everywhere, and it's neither fair nor true to say that only people who consciously deny God and affirm materialism are affected by it. Remember, materialism is the air we all breathe. Whether you like it or not, all of us live inside the materialism ecosystem, so it is not as simple as saying that religious people are happy and nonreligious people are unhappy. We all experience the effects of this ecosystem to different degrees.

The materialist story, however, cannot give you a grand enough telos to endure life under the sun. And without that type of grand telos, meaning and purpose are lost. Without meaning and purpose in life, what will you pursue? You will pursue empty things. Things that can never satisfy. Things that will turn you into the living dead.

7

Religious Materialist

YOU MIGHT RECALL WHERE THIS BOOK BEGAN, with the quote from Michael Heisman's suicide note: "If there is no extant God and no extant gods, no good and no evil, no right and no wrong, no meaning and no purpose: if there are no values that are inherently valuable; no justice that is ultimately justifiable . . . then destruction is equal to creation; life is equal to death and death is equal to life."

It's all hevel. Hevel after hevel.

There is a massive void in the materialist story that materialism can never fill. Without transcendence, without something above, we humans have a difficult time navigating our lives. We become toddlers assigning meaning to lesser things. We act like zombies, living but dead creatures looking for the smallest fix to help us cope with the pain of reality. We hunger for more but never seem to be satisfied. Countless people are living on the spectrum somewhere between toddler and zombie. Sometimes we are bits and pieces of both.

Look around and you can see the signs and symptoms everywhere. Politics has become a religion. Concerts are rituals. Sports take place in sacred time and sacred space. Everything has become religious in nature, but these things can't carry the weight assigned to them. In the materialist story, there is no father above. We are alone. We will try to find meaning and purpose in all of these lesser things, but they will always fail us. There is no stability in any of these things; they all leave us empty.

David Foster Wallace, an atheist and to many, one of the greatest authors of his generation, said:

> Because here's something else that's weird but true: in the day-to-day trenches of adult life, there is actually no such thing as atheism. There is no such thing as not worshipping. Everybody worships. The only choice we get is what to worship. And the compelling reason for maybe choosing some sort of god or spiritual-type thing to worship—be it JC or Allah, be it YHWH or the Wiccan Mother Goddess, or the Four Noble Truths, or some inviolable set of ethical principles—is that pretty much anything else you worship will eat you alive. If you worship money and things, if they are where you tap real meaning in life, then you will never have enough, never feel you have enough. It's the truth. Worship your body and beauty and sexual allure and you will always feel ugly. And when time and age start showing, you will die a million deaths before they finally grieve you. On one level, we all know this stuff already. It's been codified as myths, proverbs, clichés, epigrams, parables; the skeleton of every great story. The whole trick is keeping the truth up front in daily consciousness.[1]

In other words, even in a godless culture, we still become religious materialists. Our gods are little blankie and our next pleasure. We create structures around these gods; we have rites, rituals, and practices that encircle them. Even amid a materialist culture we will still find religious things to do.

An *Atlantic* article points out that "in an age of increasing religious disaffiliation, these (traditional) rituals now feel hollow to millions of people."[2] However, it rightly notes that people still need rituals to find meaning. It then goes on to speak of the mission of The Ritual

Design Lab. The Ritual Design Lab in Silicon Valley is a small team of "interaction designers" working to generate new rituals for modern life, with an eye to user experience.[3] The Ritual Design hotline's slogan says, "You tell us your problem. We will make you a ritual." Their website notes, "We are studying and creating rituals that bring key values to life in people's personal, work, and social circles, embodying them into how people act daily and form communities."[4]

Even when we think we have wiggled out of religion, we still end up trying to do religious things. We cannot escape rite and ritual. This is, of course, not new; there is nothing new under the sun. Probably the best example of this, and certainly a darker version of this, comes from the early days of modern materialism. The French Revolution lasted from 1789 to 1799, and in this time antireligious sentiment grew to a fever pitch. In the aptly titled "Reign of Terror," roughly three hundred thousand people were arrested, seventeen hundred were publicly executed, and as many as ten thousand died in prison or without trial.[5] Additionally, tens of thousands of clergy were exiled. In 1790 all religious orders were dissolved, and remaining clergy were made to be employees of the state.[6]

With this newfound freedom from the so-called restraints of religion, what do you suppose the newly installed leadership did after purging the land of such superstition? They set up a . . . temple. Yes, you read that right: they established a temple and dedicated it to Reason. And this was not done by one simple rogue group acting as a bad apple within the movement; there were many temples raised to honor Reason. Numerous churches were converted into temples of Reason. In fact, one of the most famous cathedrals converted was Notre-Dame.

Followers of the newly established "cult of reason" tore down and hid Christian symbols and replaced them with their own. Franklin Baumer writes, "Rising up the nave was an improvised mountain, at the top of which perched a small Greek temple dedicated 'To Philosophy' and adorned on both sides by the busts of philosophers, probably Voltaire, Rousseau, Franklin, and Montesquieu. Halfway down the side of the mountain a torch of Truth burned before an altar to Reason."[7] Liturgy was created to honor Reason, and rites and rituals were introduced. An altar to Reason was erected. And get this: this so-called religion-less people dressed up a woman in white, red, and blue and brought her into the temple. They then paid homage to her as a symbolic embodiment of the goddess of liberty.[8]

We are hopelessly religious. We humans must create rites and rituals that imbue meaning and purpose because we cannot do life without them.

MATTER MATTERS

At this point, it is important to note that the material world is important. Science matters. The laws of nature are real. But reducing all of reality to mere material origins is a grave mistake. Materialism has gone too far, trying to convince the world that materialism alone can provide the explanation for all of reality. This, however, is foolish.

Atheist Alex O'Connor, host of the *Within Reason* podcast, explains the limits of materialism well. He says:

> The mistake that [an overconfident materialism] makes is thinking that scientific laws somehow explain the universe instead of just describing them. It would be as though we discovered a book of Shakespeare's sonnets and said, "How did that get there?" And we say, "I don't know." And I start studying it and I say, "Well, look, I've just discovered like, you know, it follows this rhythm: da DA da Da da DA da Da da Da. And I'm going to call that the iambic pentameter, the law of iambic pentameter. How interesting. . . . And I've also

discovered this law, that at the end of a sentence there's usually a little dot. That's the, you know, the law of punctuation, and how after that there are two types of letters, and the big letter comes next. All these laws that I'm discovering." And [then] someone says, "Well, where did the book come from?" And you say, "Well, I don't know, we haven't answered that yet, but look at how much progress we've made in uncovering the laws of literacy. Surely one day this will . . . come to explain the origins of the literary laws themselves in the origin of the book."

O'Connor concludes, "It's a category error; it's a total mistake." One can know a book inside and out, but one's knowledge of the content of the book does not somehow do away with the need for an author.[9]

In the same conversation with Alex O'Connor, Justin Brierley, longtime host of the *Unbelievable?* podcast, repeats the words of Blaise Pascal: "Make good men wish that religion were true and then show them that it is." Brierley goes on, saying the point of this is that "we speak to people's deepest longings and desires . . . and once you maybe have shown people how they would like the world to be, then might come that logical bit [where they say], 'Well, as it turns out . . . there might be some good philosophical evidence for God.'"[10]

You long for a fair and just world. Why? You hunger for beauty, but why? You want a world that values truth over lies, but why does it matter? Where do all of these desires come from?

Love might be the greatest thing we humans experience. Are we to conclude that love can be explained away by understanding neurons, atoms, and hormones? Some will try to make this case, but it is a fool's errand.

Try telling a parent, "You don't really 'love' your child. Your relationship bond is biologically wired into you to preserve the propagation of your tribe. Also, you don't really 'love' your wife. It's just chemicals and hormones pushing you to mate to increase the chances your genetic line continues. Sure, some bonding happens along the way, but that's just biology as well."

Remember, when you set your eyes on the horizontal plane and see a beautiful sunset fleeting behind the horizon, the beauty is pointing somewhere. Look up. Follow the line. Follow its lead.

The modern world is left with a tiny truck without the power to pull the cargo that has been assigned to it. Materialism is not strong enough, whole enough, complete enough, or robust enough to carry the weight of the human experience. It just can't. A humble materialism will recognize that it cannot even explain itself.[11]

In a conversation between a comedian and a biologist, the biologist declares his belief in meaning while also holding to materialism.[12] The comedian then pushes back with a bit of humor, but also philosophical understanding. Concerning meaning, the comedian sarcastically asks the biologist, "Where does it (meaning) come from? Electromagnetism?"

What the comedian is getting at is that the things we value most as humans do not and cannot find epistemic justification within a materialist worldview. Or to say it more simply, no matter how hard we try, truth, goodness, and beauty will always point somewhere, so long as you are willing to follow their lead.

Within the boundaries of materialism one can describe nature, study its laws, and harness some of its power. But it cannot fully explain the origin and existence of nature itself. Things like love, morality, goodness, and beauty cannot be grounded within materialism's confines.

The modern person is hungry for meaning but might never bother to ask, "Where did this appetite come from?" Imagine feeling hungry and then concluding there is no such thing as food.

We hunger for meaning. We desire purpose. We long for the true, the good, and the beautiful.

People from many different walks of life are feeling the emptiness of materialism and are now realizing its insufficiency in imbuing life with meaning. We can't live life without telos. There must be more to all of this. But what is the solution? Or maybe a better question to ask is, Where does this solution come from? The answer is from above. You must look up.

We are not animals on all fours looking face-first to the earth. As humans, we stand upright. Our heads tilt toward the heavens. Like trees reaching for the sun above, we are made for more.

So far, I have been writing mostly about the problem. We have talked a lot about what's wrong and the signs and symptoms of our present ailment, but now it is time to shift. I want to talk to you from here on out not as one merely pointing to the problems but as someone who believes the Christian faith, and in particular its story accompanied with its rites, rituals, and practices, is the answer.

The good news is that there is a remedy to our ailment. There is a way out. The Christian story says that your story is not authorless. There is more than the material world. There is something above us. Truth, goodness, and beauty come from "somewhere." The truth is, we do have a Father above. The material world was created by a good God. He made and loved humanity. And even though we have made a mess of things down here, he did not abandon us to earth below. The transcendentals were always pointing to him, and when that was not enough to tilt our heads upward, the Christian story makes the radical claim that God came down to lift us up. This Father above has sent his Son; in Jesus, the transcendent becomes immanent. That which is above the sun is born beneath the sun.

In the Christian story the above and beyond come near. Two worlds come together in a person. In Jesus, we see Son of heaven and Son of earth. He is of both worlds so that he can bridge the gap. The transcendent is also *adamah*. The source of all that is good comes down. The author of our stories writes himself into our story. Jesus reveals to humanity the goodness of the Father and comes down in order that he might tilt our heads up. The Christian story says that Jesus goes to death on a cross so that death will not have the final word. The hevel of earthly life will not be the end. His cross says that your life matters. There is meaning and purpose to it.

There are many arguments that can be made and reasons that can be given to defend the Christian faith, but at the heart of the human condition is a hunger, a hunger that is answered in the Christian story.

You were made for more. More importantly, you were not merely made for more, you were made for someone. All the good that is below points to him. He is the ultimate telos. He is inevitable. We can't escape him.

> All truth is grounded here,
> All beauty finds its source here,
> All goodness is a gift from here,
> All our longings lead here,

Follow the lines, they all lead here . . . to him.

> *"You have made us for yourself, and our heart is restless until it rests in you."*
> Augustine, *Confessions*, 1.1.1.

If you want to leave behind the emptiness of materialism and escape the stale, stagnant, static, black-and-white, disenchanted world it created,

Then you must know *him*. You must know God.

Part 2

The Remedy—Belief and Embodiment

(The Wisdom of Our Ancestors)

8

To Know God

WHAT DOES IT MEAN to "know" something?

Aristotle held to three categories of knowledge: *technē* (knowledge of craft), *epistēmē* (scientific knowledge), and *phronēsis* (ethical knowledge).

In Spanish there are two words that describe two different ways of knowing: *conocer* and *saber*. *Saber* deals with information and how to do something. *Conocer*, on the other hand, has to do with places, people, and things. You can "know" how to play the guitar, but that is a different type of knowing than the way you "know" a friend. You can *saber* a guitar, but you *conocer* a friend.

In some languages, there is only one word for "know," and that word must cover a lot of ground. When this occurs, the word must be extremely flexible and able to be employed in a number of different ways. In Hebrew, the word for "know" is *yada*, and it is so flexible that in one Bible translation (English Standard Version) the word is translated in roughly twenty ways. It can mean to know something cognitively, to know something experientially, to understand something, to notice, to make known, to relationally know a friend, to have sex, and much more.

In other words, Adam may "know" his wife, and he may also "know" his wife. He may also "know" how to care for a garden and "know" that he should not eat from a certain tree. To complicate the matter, it is unclear to what degree you must "know" something before you can say, "I believe this to be true." How well do you have to play guitar before you can say, "I know how to play guitar"? Is there a difference in the degree to which you "know" an acquaintance versus a dear friend?

What is the point to all these questions? The point is that "knowing something" is quite complex and may not be as straightforward as our intuition would have us believe.

NEW KNOWLEDGE

One of the developments of the modern world has been the emphasis on factual knowledge. This is, of course, a natural consequence of the printing press, increased literacy levels, and the internet. We are all products of this massive information explosion. While acquiring new information is important, it can create a blind spot. As humans, we do not simply learn something new and then magically integrate that into the whole of our being. This might not be a big deal if, let's say, the new information is something like learning who won the most recent Super Bowl. But let's say you grew up in an environment that lacked love, and let's say you convinced yourself at an early age that the reason for that lack of love was because you were unlovable. You develop a host of fears, anxieties, and insecurities around the idea that you are not that lovable. Now imagine that you enter marriage and your spouse says, "I love you." Do you suppose you might have a hard time believing that? The answer to this is, of course, yes. Yes, it might be difficult to truly allow this newfound knowledge, that someone does indeed love you, to penetrate your inner being.

Likewise, the knowledge of Christian truth functions in a similar manner. Is God real? Is he a loving Father? Does he actually love me?

Fortunately, our spiritual ancestors created rites, rituals, and practices to reinforce our beliefs. They found ways to unite the mind, body, and spirit in a new framework. They knew you could not simply declare, "I believe in God now," and have that alone reorient your entire life. Unfortunately, the power of these rites, rituals, and practices is being forgotten.

If you finally come around to the idea that there is a transcendent being who loves you and entered into death itself to redeem you, you are going to need a whole lot of reinforcement to support that belief. The effects of materialism are strong. The good news is that the church has long guarded these methods and kept them secure. These support structures are found in the rites, rituals, and practices of the Christian faith. The church knew that belief needed more support than just an initial affirmation of faith. The bad news is that even though these practices have been kept secure, they are like an old diamond ring kept in a safe: secure, yes, but not on display for the world to see. And even when we take the diamond ring out to look at it, we may not have the eye to truly appreciate the beauty we have in our possession.

EMBODIED CREATURES

Human beings are embodied creatures. We have bodies and we live and learn and breathe in those bodies. Belief, therefore, if it is truly going to transform all of who we are, must be embodied as well. Materialism says you are just a body; the Christian faith says you are a physical and spiritual being. Understanding this enables us to have a whole and complete picture of who we are.

In the book of Acts, one of the first Christians, named Peter, gives a presentation of the Christian gospel message. Upon hearing the message and listening to the information contained therein, the listeners ask: "What shall we do?" Look carefully at how Peter responds:

"Repent and be baptized" (Acts 2:37-38).

Did you catch that? Peter did not say, "You now have nothing more to do, for the information is now contained in your minds."

He said they must now be baptized. What, then, is baptism? Baptism is a ritual in which you reenact the death and resurrection of Jesus in your body. You go down into the water (death) and come up out of the water (with new life). This is incredibly profound. In baptism, in your body, you are dramatizing the death and resurrection of Jesus and applying it to your life. The story is told in your very flesh; the act itself is storytelling. The narrative takes its shape in your body.

Why is this important? Because we are embodied creatures. We are not just a mind. Human beings don't simply say, "I love you." We hug, we embrace, we kiss. On a wedding day the climax of the ceremony is the moment right after the minister says, "You may now kiss the bride."

When a child knows they have done something wrong, it is not until they begin to open their mouth and say, "I am sorry," that the tears begin to flow. The state of being sorry is already there, but it is not until it is manifested by the body that the tears begin to come. If we are going to counter the materialist story that we have been living inside, we must believe *and* embody the Christian story at every level. Both body and spirit—and their connection—matter.

In the Hebrew scriptures, there is a book filled with 150 songs famously known as the book of Psalms. In the Seventy-Third Psalm, there is a psalmist who looks out at the world and becomes extremely depressed. He observes all the suffering and injustice in the world, and it overwhelms him. In his eyes, the wicked seem to prosper and the innocent suffer. His faith begins to fail.

Have you been there? Have you ever turned on the news and seen so much bad news that you begin to question everything? You question how you live, how you ought to live, and maybe even question what you think about God. Psalm 73 is right there with you.

The author of Psalm 73 does something remarkable at this point, however. Rather than sulk in his feelings, he goes somewhere— somewhere specific. He goes to the temple. And when the psalmist goes to the temple, something remarkable happens. All his thoughts and feelings are reordered and restructured. It is not as if he acquires new knowledge or receives new information; rather, he experiences a reordering of all that he already knew. Even more fascinating, this was done not by some secret inward journey but by an embodied action. He goes to the temple, and the temple, with all its structure, adornments, signs, and symbols, takes existing knowledge and reorders it in such a way that the psalmist can say:

> But when I thought how to understand this,
>   it seemed to me a wearisome task,
> until I went into the sanctuary of God;
>   then I discerned their end. (Psalm 73:16-17)

The psalmist goes from his soul being embittered to speaking of the reality and goodness of God. Why is this so significant? Did the psalmist learn something new at the temple? Did someone at the temple install new curtains with new symbols, and it suddenly made the psalmist realize something? Was the incense different that day? The answer is, of course, no. The psalmist's entire self was reoriented toward true reality, and this was done by the *physical act* of going to the temple.

SEVEN PRACTICES

In the second portion of this book, I want to get extremely practical. Up to this point, we have navigated the waters of materialism and seen how they create a world without meaning and purpose. An authorless story and a fatherless world are soul crushing. Breathing the air of that ecosystem makes us sick. To remedy this, we made the turn and said that if we want to recover meaning and purpose, then we must follow the lines and look up.

At this point it will not be enough to say that the answer is simply to "believe in God," as if there were a light switch that you could flip on and instantly have cognitive certainty of who you are, why you matter, and the reality of God. Yes, you must believe in God, but that belief needs to be strengthened with the proper support. We must learn to live inside the Christian story and act it out. Our bodies must redramatize the story and the tenets of the Christian faith.

The modern world often loses sight of much of what kept the faith alive in so many people throughout the centuries. We often have made faith into something that is done mostly "in our mind" and "in our heart." We have made it about going deeper and deeper inside ourselves, yet the Christian faith travels not only inward but also outward. The Christian faith is an embodied faith. After all, the central claim of Christianity is that a dead man came back to life in the flesh.

Our ancestors in the faith believed in their hearts and minds, but they also believed with their bodies. They acted out the faith. They knew life under the sun was a difficult one, and so they fortified their belief with structure. This structure is the rites, rituals, and practices of the first Christians.

In part two, we will look at seven practices of the church. These seven are not exhaustive, but these seven are foundational. These practices work as the remedy to the effects of materialism. They fill in the blanks of the true story of the world and orient us in it. They give us a new ecosystem to live and breathe in. They tell us who we are, where we are, and when we are. They fix our gaze upward. They help us rightly order our lives. They strengthen us for the harshness of life. They give us belonging. They give us aim, direction, and purpose. They bring us telos. A life of meaning and fullness is found in them.

What materialism has robbed, these seven practices now return.

9

Song

BY THIS POINT, you are probably excited to discover these secret, ancient, life-changing practices. Well, I'd like to start with one that seems so common, so mundane, that my guess is that you are going to be disappointed at first.

Let's talk about singing.

For thousands of years, our ancestors sang. Singing is one of those things we all just sort of do, but rarely do we stop to think about what is happening when we do it. It is so ubiquitous that many modern people have forgotten the power contained in song. When we sing, something is taking place, something far more profound than we have allowed ourselves to believe. For lack of a better term, it's magic. Singing is magic.

Our spiritual ancestors believed in the power of song. They sang songs of earth's beginning, of mighty acts of deliverance, of suffering and triumph. Singing is a way to embody sacred truth in the very fabric of our being. Humans can play a guitar or piano, but when we sing, we are transforming our bodies into a living, walking, breathing instrument. When we sing, and especially when we sing matters of sacred truth, we are reorienting our internal compass; we are recalibrating how we navigate the world. We allow the true story of the world to find shape in the words of our songs. We are literally pointing our entire being at ultimate reality, and allowing it to conform us to it. How in the world does this happen? Let's examine the building blocks of this phenomenon and see how much we have been missing.

What is a musical note? When someone plucks a guitar string, the string begins to vibrate. The rate of vibration will be determined by several factors, such as what the string is made of, how long the string is, and how tightly the string is being pulled. On a guitar, the low E string vibrates at a rate of 82 times per second, and the high E string vibrates at a rate of 330 times per second. The middle C note on a piano will vibrate at a rate of 256 times per second. This vibration produces what we call a musical note. You might ask, "How does a vibrating string create a sound that we perceive as a musical note?"

It is quite remarkable what occurs immediately after the string begins to vibrate. Air particles pick up the vibration pattern and are pushed out of the guitar's resonant chamber. These air particles then bump into other air particles that, in turn, pick up that same vibration pattern and collide with other air particles. This process continues until eventually those vibrations make it to your ear. Inside your ear, the vibrations are detected by tiny hair-like fibers found in a small part of your body called the cochlea. It is here that those vibrations are converted into an electrical signal and then sent to the brain and processed as sound. Invisible air particles fly around at the speed of sound and find their way to a tiny opening in the human body where they are converted into an electrical signal—all so that we can hear the hum of an E string on a guitar.

Magic, right? Just wait, we are only getting started.

When a human being begins to sing, much like a guitar string, their vocal cords begin to vibrate. If you want to sing well and on key, then your vocal cords better be vibrating at the right frequency. So, if you want to sing a middle C note, then your vocal cords need to be vibrating at 256 times per second. As your vocal cords vibrate at these incredibly fast speeds, the sound they make is then amplified and shaped by resonators in your body, including your chest, nasal passages, throat, mouth, and even your bones and skull.[1]

These resonators enhance the energy they receive from your vibrating vocal cords; your entire being participates in this act and your very body becomes a natural amplifier. Along the way, these resonators add their unique touch by shaping the timbre of the notes produced, causing everyone to have their own unique voice.

In the same way a guitar string is plucked on an acoustic guitar and the wooden chamber amplifies the energy of the original note, so you, too, in your flesh and in your bones, amplify the sound your brain tells your vocal cords to make. When a mother sings a lullaby over her child, her entire person is singing comfort over her baby. Deep in her soul, she makes melody; her brain sends the needed information to her body, her flesh and bones vibrate with the music from deep in her innermost, she opens her mouth and lets out that which is unseen to the eye, and within the blink of an eye begins to soothe her crying child.

Magic, right?

SING TOGETHER

"[Speak] to one another with psalms, hymns, and songs from the Spirit. Sing and make music from your heart to the Lord" (Ephesians 5:19 NIV).

One of the first leaders in the early Christian movement was a man named Paul. In a letter he wrote to Christians, he encouraged them to sing with each other and to each other. More specifically, he told them not just to sing any old song but to center their singing on the Lord. This instruction, of course, flows from his ancestors, as Paul was a Jewish man who grew up with the songbook of Psalms that we previously discussed. Since the birth of the church, Christians have always gathered together to sing songs to God. This prompts the question: What happens when we do this?

Oxytocin is a hormone that is produced in the hypothalamus and released into the bloodstream by the pituitary gland.[2] It is often referred to as the "love hormone," "cuddle hormone," "kiss hormone," and even the "sex hormone," among other names. The reason for these names is derived from oxytocin's function. Oxytocin is released when we engage in a romantic kiss or are embraced in the hug of a loved one. It is also released in massive amounts during childbirth; the hormone helps create one of the most powerful bonds that humans experience, the bond between a mother and her newborn child.

There is another action that causes oxytocin to be released, and do you want to take a guess at what that is? Yes, that's right: singing. When you sing, oxytocin is released, and research shows that overall happiness is increased, and worry and sadness decrease.[3] Your body has a natural, God-given mechanism to help you toil through life. Maybe this is why so many people learn to sing in their morning showers. They have unknowingly developed a habit that helps them cope with the harshness of life. Singing helps you survive.

What happens when we sing with others? Oxytocin is released, and we bond with those singing with us. When we sing with others, we are not only getting the benefit of increased happiness, but we are also sharing that experience with others. Having that same experience strengthens relational bonds. On top of that, research shows that in choirs, the heartbeats of the singers even begin to sync up.[4] When we sing with other people, our bodies center themselves on the rhythm, melody, and tempo of a song we are all collectively orienting ourselves toward. Our breathing changes, our heartbeat changes, our feelings change . . . we change. Magic, right?

Part of the reason we are missing out on so much of this is because our culture has less and less space where people have regular rhythms of gathering to sing together. Think about it, we have headphones and Spotify and Bluetooth speakers. For the first time in human history, we are experiencing music alone. For all of human history, music was always performed live and in person. There was no such thing as recorded music.

What a strange place we find ourselves in now. Sure, we may go to a concert every now and then or take our chance at karaoke, but for many people, music is primarily experienced alone and through recordings. Making matters even more unique, we have access to pretty much the sum total of all recorded music at our fingertips. You can listen to whatever you want, whenever you want. That is a world of difference from having a set book of Psalms which you sing from over and over again. We have music preferences. We can choose from any genre we want. However, there was a time when your personal preference for music was completely irrelevant to what you heard and sang. You simply gathered and sang the songs you always sang. Music, with all its beauty and wonder, was, up until yesterday, never done alone.

There is a place, however, where regular, performed, in-person music takes place among a collected group. One day every week there is a place where people can gather to sing together. Like the diamond hidden in a closet safe, there is something precious to rediscover.

CHURCH MUSIC

So far, we have discussed what happens when you sing, and what happens when you sing with others. Now let's complete the triad and talk about what is happening when you do this and direct your songs to God.

If you were to walk into a church on a Sunday morning, you might hear lyrics such as "No power of hell, no scheme of man, Can ever pluck me from His hand."[5] Or "Holy, Holy, Holy, Lord

God Almighty,"[6] or something like: "Then sings my soul, my Savior God to Thee, How great Thou art, how great Thou art."[7]

Church songs are songs that speak of that which is most high. They do not speak of lesser things. Singing of lesser things, like love, romance, or having a "good time," are not bad in and of themselves; they just are not the same thing as church music. Songs dedicated to God are in a different category. They are different kinds of songs. Church songs establish true north. They are telling you what matters most, what to fix your gaze on, what you should chiefly value. They remind you that there is a being whose truth, goodness, and beauty are beyond measure.

The problem is most of the music we sing does not fall into this category. The songs of our culture are fixated on lesser things, and if a culture's entire song catalog is void of God, then that culture will end up making these lesser things ultimate things. This is exactly what we are doing. We elevate common music to the level of worship music and end up singing to lesser things as if they were God. Unknowingly, we have praise and worship music in our playlists; it's just that the songs are dedicated to love, sex, romance, power, and sometimes even just having a "good time."

Listen to the music of our culture and see what comes out. Time and time again, you will hear people, things, and experiences elevated to some transcendent level. It is as if we are trying to create a religious experience out of irreligious material. It's little blankie music. It's remarkable when you think about it. As a society, we are so bent against religion that we kick it out of our songs, only then to unknowingly try and create religious experiences out of our so-called nonreligious life.

This is seen in countless songs, but one that illustrates this amazingly well is "E.T." by Katy Perry.[8] The song is about a romantic relationship that leads to a sexual encounter. Singing about sex is nothing new, but the way in which she describes the romantic encounter is fascinating. In the pre-chorus, she sings of the romance being from a "different dimension" and how the romance redirects her eyes and leads her "into the light."

Already, you have the building blocks for a religious song that you could sing at a church. The song is describing a "love" from some other world or transcendent place. This relationship has the power to "open . . . eyes" and bring you "into the light." These are lyrics of salvation. These are lyrics using the language of morality; to be brought into the light is to speak in the ethical dimension. The song continues in the chorus with a request for a kiss, followed by lyrics describing the sexual encounter as "supernatural" and "extraterrestrial."

At this point, what's happening here is beginning to become clear. In the absence of God and religious categories, we still cannot shake the need for transcendent experiences, so we end up trying to make the natural, supernatural. The boy is described as being from another world, a supernatural world. The bridge goes on: "This is transcendental . . . for you, I'll risk it all."

At this point, it's on the nose, right? Romance, relationship, and sex are the transcendent experience. This experience comes from another world, and it is so good we will risk our life for it. What ends up happening when we center all of our songs on such things is that we create objects of devotion. We use romance as a life compass. We make sex our true north. We try to find meaning and purpose in sexual experience. We allow lesser things to be the wind captured in the sails.

Again, there is nothing wrong with singing about these lesser things, but everything has to be in proper order. Only a transcendent being can carry the weight of transcendence. The songs of our culture cannot do what we want them to do. Our playlists cannot anchor us in the storm. They are not weighty enough to sink deep enough and catch the ocean floor. And this brings us back to the music we sing as a gathered people unto God.

A SONG FOR EVERY BATTLE

When you sing songs at church, you sing songs that you have sung time and time again. You memorize the words and melodies. The lyrics repaint reality so that whatever happened to you during the week, you are reminded of the truth, goodness, and beauty of the only one worthy of worship. When you begin to open your mouth, you are not merely singing a song. You are singing of ultimate things; you are singing of transcendent power. You are reorienting your entire being on that which is most true. You are fixing your gaze on true north. You are making your entire being an instrument of truth, goodness, and beauty. The reality of God is resonating in your very flesh and bones.

As you do so, your body vibrates and amplifies these truths. Your body, in response to what it is doing, releases hormones that are delivering you joy and uniting you with the other participants in the room. Individually, your body becomes a part of a larger body, which then collectively sings of holy, sacred, and transcendent realities. You are taking what you believe on the inside and manifesting it to the outside world.

It is not enough to say that you believe in God. That will not sustain you when life hits you like a freight train. You must embody that belief—not because it will justify your belief before God, but because you need it. Every ounce of who you are needs it.

You may have confessed belief in God and even spoken about the love of a heavenly Father, but if you are honest with yourself, there are some days when you just don't feel it. There are some days when you *feel* so distant and so far from the ideas that you say you believe. In those moments, remember there is a way to *feel* those beliefs materially, tangibly, and physically in your very flesh and bones. Counter the lie of materialism with songs of truth, goodness, and beauty. Allow the truths from heaven to come down and take residence in your body. You are, after all, made to be an instrument of praise. Whatever life throws at you, you have songs to fight the falsehoods you might be tempted to adopt.

When you are reminded of the fact that your own earthly father left you and you are feeling the overwhelming weight of thinking you have always been unlovable, do not for a second believe that lie. Remind yourself of what is ultimately true about who you are, align yourself with true north, and sing: "How deep the Father's love for us, How vast beyond all measure."[9]

When you receive bad news from the doctor, sing: "No power of hell, no scheme of man, Can ever pluck me from His hand."[10]

When the guilt and shame of yesterday comes back to haunt you and you feel unworthy, sing: "Amazing grace, how sweet the sound."[11]

When you look out at the world and become stressed out of your mind, sing: "This is my Father's world, why should my heart be sad?"[12]

When you lose your job and are terrified about finances, lift your hands and sing: "Riches I heed not, nor man's empty praise, thou mine inheritance now and always."[13]

Sing of his great mercy and love. Embody these invisible and sacred truths and make your temple a resonate chamber of heaven. You need it, and the person next to you needs it. Proclaim these sacred truths: There is a God. He is your Father. And he loves you beyond measure.

TASTE AND SEE

In Psalm 34:8, King David says, "Oh, taste and see that the LORD is good." What is fascinating about this verse is the language used. *Taste* and *see* are sensory words. They are words used to describe the body's activities. Likewise, the Bible says on many occasions to clap, shout, sing, and make a joyful noise to the Lord (Psalms 47:1; 98:4; 100:1; Isaiah 12:5-6). Again and again we see that the immaterial God is meant to be worshiped and experienced with our material bodies, and if that is the case, it is because God himself designed our bodies to work in this manner.

God gave us the gift of music and he gave us the gift of worship. When we combine the two, the entire human person is brought into something that is truly supernatural. Music with others, directed as praise to God, changes us; it changes us from the inside out. It changes us both as individuals and as a group. Songs directed upward to God push back the poisonous air of materialism. The trillions of cells that form our one body are united in the act of song, and our one body joins the group of worshippers and forms a larger body. We unite in body, soul, and spirit, and we project out into this world truths from another world. It really is magical.

So, does the weight of the world have you down? Is your faith feeling a little shaky? Are you telling yourself you will never be good enough? Are you wondering if you matter and if your life has any real meaning? If so, go to church and sing. Sing as if singing will help you survive the harshness of the world, because it will. Sing as if your life depended on it, because it does.

Come, taste and see that the Lord is good.

10

Baptism

AS WE LOOK AT MORE OF THE RITES, rituals, and practices of our spiritual ancestors, I'd like to expand on one previously mentioned: baptism. What is baptism and what is it doing?

Baptism is storytelling.

But the storytelling takes place not with words but with our entire body. Like fingers on a typewriter pressing letters on paper that produce the story, so the body is forming the syllables that tell the story. The entire narrative structure of the gospel finds shape and form in human flesh. Every time an individual is baptized, the gospel is told.

How does this work?

Before we speak of how the gospel is told in baptism, it is important to know what the gospel actually is. We already covered this a bit at the conclusion of chapter seven, but I want to get a little more specific here. The Greek word that is translated "gospel" in the New Testament is *euangelion*. Euangelion simply means "good news." So, whatever the gospel is, it is fundamentally news that is good. Additionally, news is not advice, nor a process, nor some journey you must go on; news is something that happened. When you read the news, you are reading a report on what has already occurred.

The next question is this: What is the content of this news? The good news is the victory of Jesus over Satan, sin, and death . . . achieved by his life, death, and resurrection.

So, when the New Testament authors speak of the gospel, they are speaking of this. Now there is much more that can be said, and innumerable implications of the gospel, but this understanding will suffice for a basic understanding.

How then does baptism proclaim this gospel? To understand this, we need to go back and look at how the first Christians viewed baptism. For them, the story of the life, death, and resurrection of Jesus is embedded into baptism at every level. Paul the apostle wrote, "Do you not know that all of us who have been baptized into Christ Jesus were baptized into his death? We were buried therefore with him by baptism into death, in order that, just as Christ was raised from the dead by the glory of the Father, we too might walk in newness of life" (Romans 6:3-4).

Paul is saying that when a person goes into the waters, they go into a type of death. And when they rise, they come up in a type of new life. Additionally, when they go into that death, it is not as if they go alone—Paul says they are buried *with Jesus*. Likewise, just as Jesus is raised, so too are they raised. In other words, going under the waters is going into death with Jesus, and coming out of the waters is coming up into new life alongside the resurrected Jesus. Baptism is not just about *representation*, it's about *participation*. We go down with Jesus and come up with Jesus. When we are baptized, our story is bound to his story.

If our bodies, then, are telling the story of Christ going into death and rising, then in every baptism there is a proclaiming of the gospel message. Our bodies are the vehicle by which the narrative is proclaimed. Not with words but in a type of sign language. The signs are communicated not with our hands but with the sum of our physical being. First, we believe the gospel, it takes root in our innermost, and then we proclaim the gospel in our bodies, manifesting its truth in the material world.

Every baptism is a retelling of the greatest story ever told.

Baptism was so important to the first Christians that it was always considered essential for everyone who confessed the name of Jesus. Fast forward two thousand years and it can often seem like baptism is optional. It's something that's available to Christians who want to take the "next step." For the first Christians, however, baptism was never the next step; it was always the first step.

JUST BELIEVE IN YOUR HEART?

"Want to become a Christian?" the preacher asks. "Just believe in your heart that Jesus died on the cross for your sins and rose on the third day, and you shall be saved. That's it. That's all you must do. The Bible says it's that simple—believe in your heart."

But is that all you must do? Just believe in your heart?

Well, sort of . . .

The verse that says, "Believe in your heart and you shall be saved," also says, "If you confess with your mouth that Jesus is Lord, then you shall be saved." Here is the exact wording:

"If you confess with your mouth that Jesus is Lord and believe in your heart that God raised him from the dead, you will be saved" (Romans 10:9).

Wait a second, this verse says you also must confess with your mouth. So, what do you have to do to get saved? Just believe? Or do you need to confess out loud that Jesus is Lord? What if there is no one there to hear you confess? Do you need a minimum number of people there to hear you confess?

Let's make it even more complicated. In the book of Acts, the apostle Peter gives the first post-resurrection gospel message, and after the people hear his words, they ask, "What should we do?" The crowd wants to know how they ought to respond to the gospel. Peter answers, "*Repent and be baptized* every one of you in the name of Jesus Christ for the forgiveness of your sins" (Acts 2:38, italics added).

So again, what do you have to do to be saved? Just believe? Confess out loud? Repent? Get baptized? Is it all four? Does it count if you do two out of the four?

To be clear, I do believe that the internal faith of the individual is what saves. We are saved by God's grace, received through faith (Ephesians 2:8-9). But I do want to point out that the Bible seems not to separate internal belief from something immediately done with the body—namely, baptism.

The Bible, along with most ancient people, knew that we need to do things with our bodies. We need to say things out loud. We need to stand in reverence. We need to bow our heads. Belief is reinforced when it materializes in the physical world with the whole of our being: heart-mind-body.

Because of this, initial faith was never separated from baptism. The waters of baptism were the natural stream flowing from the initial source of faith. Grace saves, through faith, but out of faith flows obedience in baptism.

SIGNS AND SACRAMENTS

Since the very beginning, nearly every church in history has believed that baptism was a sacrament. It was the action you did with your body to communicate your faith in Jesus and thus gave you entry into the church body. What is a sacrament? The Bible does not give us a precise definition, but various theologians have made attempts. One definition that is often used is "an outward sign of an inward grace." The Westminster Shorter Catechism, written in 1647, states, "A sacrament is a holy ordinance instituted by Christ; wherein, by sensible signs, Christ, and the benefits of the new covenant, are represented, sealed, and applied to believers."[1] In other words, a sacrament is something done in the material world that imparts the blessings of Christ. It is important to note that a sacrament is instituted by Christ. It is not some new spiritual practice promising new benefits. It is of divine origin. A sacrament comes from God.

For all of Christian history, the church believed that doing something with your body was extremely important. The modern world often values the inside more than the outside. We seem to value what's in the heart most of all. So, it is no coincidence that we have so emphasized what's on the inside that sometimes what's on the outside is lost.

If you grew up in a Christian home, you will know exactly what I'm talking about in the following example. Picture that hypothetical preacher mentioned earlier in this chapter asking people if they want to become a Christian and get saved. Usually, after he tells them that all they must do is "believe in your heart," something more is offered. He goes on, "The Bible says you must believe in your heart that Jesus died and rose for your sins. So, in a moment, I am going to pray, and with every eye closed and every head bowed, I'd like you to say this prayer in the quietness of your heart: Dear Jesus, I know I am a sinner, and that you died on the cross for my sins and on the third day rose. I confess you as Lord and Savior of my life. I invite you into my heart."

This prayer comes in many different shapes and sizes, but the fundamentals are all the same. These fundamentals are so clear that if you grew up in church, no matter the variation of how the prayer is given, you know this prayer as the "Sinner's Prayer." There is nothing wrong with a heartfelt prayer asking Jesus into one's life. The problem lies elsewhere. Namely, the "Sinner's Prayer" has replaced baptism as the sacrament that initiates someone in the faith, and baptism has been downgraded to something you do when you are ready to "take your faith more seriously." Again, in the Bible, baptism is not the *next* step; it is the *first* step.

A prayer declaring faith in Jesus is great, but that should be followed by the rite that Jesus commanded. It is extremely important that we have faith on "the inside." But remember, the Christian faith always travels in two directions: inward and outward to the world. We believe in our hearts, confess with our mouths, and with our bodies go into the waters.

For that matter, it is our external actions that demonstrate what our internal beliefs and commitments are. Listen to the words of Jesus when he confronted Christians who had a problem of the heart: "But I have this against you, that you have abandoned the love you had at first. Remember therefore from where you have fallen; repent, and do the works you did at first" (Revelation 2:4-5).

The Christians in a church in the first century had lost their first love. For these Christians it was an issue of the heart. But pay close attention to what Jesus says. He tells them to remember, repent, and then *do the works you did at first*. Did you catch that? Do the things you first did. In other words, when our actions do not align with what we say is in our heart, it is likely because something with our heart is at fault. Our actions, put on display externally, reflect what is internally in our hearts. Jesus does not tell this church, "Return to your first love and feel the things you first felt." He says, "Return to your first love and *do the things you first did*." Your actions demonstrate the true state of your heart. So yes, what you believe in your heart matters, but only inasmuch as that faith manifests in the real, external world.

Imagine a husband who displays no outward love for his wife. He does not work, he does not do any household chores, he never remembers birthdays and anniversaries, never expresses thankfulness, and at best manages to fit in a shower every couple of days. After years of this behavior getting worse, his wife finally asks, "Do you even still love me?" The husband looks confused and responds, "Babe, uh, yeah, of course I love you. I have tons of love for you." Then, pointing to his heart, he says, "It's all in here, baby, so much love, all in my heart. If you could just see all the love in my heart, you would know."

Well, there is a way to see into someone's heart: by seeing how they live. Listen to Jesus: "If you love me, you will keep my commandments" (John 14:15). Love will change our behavior. Of course, we will never obey Christ's commands perfectly, and none of us will ever be an absolutely perfect spouse; nevertheless, the love and desires of our hearts will pull our actions in a direction that embodies what we claim is on the inside.

Faith must never reside only in the heart; it must be proclaimed, and initial saving faith is proclaimed in the drama of baptism.

Important to note, it is not as though God is bound to make us use the physical acts of rite and ritual. It is, however, for our good that God has commissioned them. He knows us, he made us, and he knows that these things mold and shape us. Baptism is a gift.

But this gift is also a commitment, one that needs to be made in front of witnesses. We need to feel the water rush over our heads. We need to rise out of the water, open our eyes, and see the church family we now belong to, smiling back at us. Promises made in our hearts are easily broken. Public professions are much stronger. And this gets us to another point of utmost importance: baptism is a public pledge of allegiance.

PLEDGING ALLEGIANCE

Very early in church history we have records indicating that when new Christians were baptized, part of the ceremony was a renouncing of Satan, demons, and the world. An early Christian leader by the name of Tertullian wrote, "When we are going to enter the water, but a little before, in the presence of the congregation and under the hand of the president, we solemnly profess that we disown the devil, and his pomp, and his angels."[2] In a third-century church handbook, it is recorded: "Then the presbyter, taking hold of each of those about to be baptized, shall command him to renounce, saying: I renounce thee, Satan, and all thy servants and all thy works."[3]

Formulas like these are found throughout church history.[4] The first Christians knew that baptism was an act that elevated Christ to the highest position. If there were any allegiances higher than him, they needed to be renounced. A formal denunciation was required. Like being sworn in to the military or receiving citizenship to a country you were not born in, there were words that were spoken to indicate what commitments had been made.

Baptism thus brings us into the people of God in a formal sense. It is an act that binds our story with Christ's story and his church. We are declaring that we are aligned with Christ in his life and death, and he has our total allegiance. His story is our story.

And this gets us to a massive problem the modern person faces. In the materialist story of the world, there is no ultimate allegiance given, and thus no organizing principle. So priorities, commitments, and values have no hierarchy to sit in. They are like single puzzle pieces that are incapable of forming a whole picture. They are floating fragments, lacking the grounding needed to build a structure. It is nearly impossible to live like that. Baptism reminds us of ultimate things and provides the proper hierarchy of values to order our lives. What do I mean by this? The church father Augustine wrote:

> But living a just and holy life requires one to be capable of an objective and impartial evaluation of things: to love things, that is to say, in the right order, so that you do not love what is not to be loved, or fail to love what is to be loved, or have a greater love for what should be loved less, or an equal love for things that should be loved less or more, or a lesser or greater love for things that should be loved equally.[5]

We must love things in the right order; otherwise, we will love some things too much and others too little. We might call the levels at which we love things our hierarchy of values. Think of it as a triangle. At the very top is the thing we value and love most. As we move down the triangle, the triangle gets wider, and we place things there that we value less. This does not necessarily mean we have little love for them; it just means they are subordinate to the things above them.

What we love and value determines how we live. For thousands of years, humans looked to religion to give them a system that ordered their lives. For example, a knight in the Middle Ages might say he loves God, king, and kingdom, in that order. A peasant farmer in early America might say he loves God, family, and country, in that order.

Religion has typically given people a structure in which to order the various components of their life. This is true in Islam, Hinduism, Judaism, and other religions. In Christianity, the top of the hierarchy is reserved for God alone. *You shall have no other gods before me.* God must sit at the top as the highest love in one's life.

This is not to say that other loves are unimportant. These loves are not lost. In fact, they are amplified when properly ordered. For example, a husband does not love his wife less because he loves God most. When properly ordered, a man's love for God strengthens and reinforces his love for his wife. How? Because God himself has commanded husbands to love their wives. In loving her, he not only honors her, but he honors God as well.

Parents should love their children, but again in the right order. If they put their kids at the top of their hierarchy of values, things will go terribly wrong. Children can be elevated above God, and that is extremely dangerous. You might say, "What's wrong with a parent loving their kids most of all? Is God so selfish or insecure that he demands we love him more than we love our own kids?"

Remember, God is the source of all goodness, and whatever comes from him is good. This means that his commands are good. It is not as if the cosmic father in the sky is so demanding he would request proper love for children as a sacrifice in order that he might be properly worshiped. It is, in fact, the opposite: love of God preserves children from being sacrificed.

Putting your children at the top of your hierarchy of values will ultimately lead to destruction in their life and yours. How? You are putting the weight of functioning as god on the lap of your children. Your children cannot bear the weight of being your Lord and Savior. They cannot bear the weight of such an assignment. They deserve properly ordered love and deserve not to have that pressure put on their back.

If your kids are at the top of your hierarchy of values, you will smother them. You will weigh them down. You will overprotect them. You will not raise them in a manner that enables them to become mature adults capable of leaving home and facing the world. You will keep them as children. God at the top of the hierarchy is not at odds with love of children. Children will be loved all the more with proper ordering.

Think also about the importance people place on career. Careers are great, but they, too, can become gods. Imagine a man who has been convinced his career is the most important thing in his life. He will do anything to climb the ranks of the corporate ladder. He will stay late and work hard and go the extra mile. In the right order, hard work is a good thing. But in the wrong order, it's devastating.

Imagine this same man has a loving wife and three kids at home. He grew up being bullied and was never part of the "cool group" at school. He was always on the outside, even sitting by himself at lunch. When he got out of college, he landed the dream job. He loves his wife and kids, but he also desperately wants people to respect him, to see him as the winner he never was as a kid.

He begins making money, experiences much success, and climbs the ranks at work. He is no longer the loser kid who ate lunch alone. He does, however, now work so hard that he is rarely home for dinner. Over time, the lure of success hooked him into placing his career at the top of his hierarchy of values.

He becomes a bad husband and a bad father, willingly sacrificing his family on the altar of a successful career. His god is his success. And he daily goes to the temple of success and sacrifices his family. A religious structure is always at work.

A RIGHTLY ORDERED LIFE

The modern person living in the materialist story of the world finds themselves in a conundrum when trying to create a hierarchy of values. What should go on top? And most importantly, why should it go on top?

In a completely materialist system, where do we look to order our values? Worse still, can values even exist in that type of system? Is it just subjective and individually determined based on personal preference? What should we most value? Should following our heart be our chief value? Should education? Career? Love? Family? Country? Sex? Why not video games?

It's not only what's at the top of the triangle that needs a proper place in the hierarchy. Take, for example, giving to the poor. Does charity to those in need matter? Is it a valuable endeavor? If so, to what degree? Should one sacrifice their own pleasure so others might have more? Should one care for the needs of others as their own? Again, if so, why?

Why does it matter that people are in need? What ethical demands are placed on us to care? What value do they hold for us? Can't we just care for the poor in our heart? That's what really matters, right? Or does demonstrable action to care for those in need have value? And if so, where does that value come from?

Modern people living in the materialist story can find themselves feeling like a big ball of knots, contradictions, and tensions. We have no objective value system that governs our lives, and so we live completely disordered and contradictory lives.

Look around at the countless plans, routines, and apps we have promising to give some sort of order to a particular area of our life. We have thousands of diet plans, workout routines, finance trackers, dating algorithms, even apps that remind us to breathe . . . all helping us to try and bring a little structure to any given area of our life, all the while our life as a whole has no organizing principle.

The first step in creating order in one's life is identifying what sits at the top. What do you love most? What do you desire most? What is most valuable? Where do you look for meaning, purpose, and direction? If one does not have a principle at the top, chaos ensues below. In the disorder of a hierarchy, there can be no unity of being. Fitness, romance, money, family, friendship, leisure time, and everything else will better find their proper place when you know what they sit under.

Baptism is the formal ceremony by which we put Christ at the top of the hierarchy. All former allegiances are either renounced or put in their proper subordinate positions. The Scriptures, then, outline the commands of Jesus and begin to create a structure for values to find their appropriate location.

First, "Love the LORD your God with all your heart and with all your soul and with all your might" (Deuteronomy 6:5). Love of God is a vertical love. We look up. Our neck tilts and our eyes are fixed to heaven. It is from this chief love that rests above that we are then directed to love in the horizontal.

Second, "Love your neighbor as yourself" (Mark 12:31). How ought we love others in the horizontal? Well, again, the Bible speaks to all of this. Love of spouse matters (Ephesians 5:28). Love of children matters (Psalm 127:3). Love of family matters (1 Timothy 5:7-8). Love of those in need matters (James 1:27). Love of other Christians matters (Matt 25:40). Not just people, but things matter. Food and drink are good (Deuteronomy 14:26); they are gifts from God but must be in right order. Romance and sex are gifts (Proverbs 5:15-19), but they need to be put in the right order.

Baptism swears allegiance to Christ as chief love in our life, thus enabling us to begin to organize everything in its right order according to its right value, under him and according to him. That which sits on top determines the order and structure of everything below. If Christ is at the top of the hierarchy, then we can begin to love things in the right manner.

So, let's put all of this together and ask once again, "What is baptism and what is it doing?"

Baptism is storytelling. It's not only telling the story of Christ but also telling your story. You now live inside of its narrative structure. Your feet do not wander aimlessly on a planet that wanders aimlessly throughout a universe void of purpose. You have sworn allegiance in your heart, mind, and body. You have a Father who sent his Son to die for you. You have been buried with him. You rise with him. You have a purpose in life: to serve the One who sits at the top of the hierarchy, your King and Lord.

Baptism answers the question, To whom do you belong? You belong to him.

His story is your story.

11

Communion

WHERE ARE YOU? Pretty simple answer, right? You might be reading this book in your room, an office, or maybe even under the noonday sun at the park. It's a pretty straightforward answer to a simple question. Try this one:

When are you?

A bit tougher, right? Well, in some sense, it's still easy. You can look at your phone for the time or at a calendar for the date, but I'm asking for something much deeper than that. To what time do you belong?

In the time of Jesus, a possible answer to this question would have been the *olam hazeh*, which translates from Hebrew to English as "the present age." This contrasts with the *olam haba*, which means "the age to come." In order to understand the olam hazeh and the olam haba, we have to understand the way people in Jesus' time and place looked at the world. So let's go back a little more than two thousand years, to the time leading up to the birth of Jesus.

In this period, the Jewish people presupposed that the present age was an evil time. All they had to do was look around to come to that conclusion. An oppressive empire controlled the land, tyrants ruled the day, and the Messiah had not come. For hundreds of years their people suffered under the Assyrians, the Babylonians, the Greeks, and now Rome. If anyone dared challenge the might of

Rome, they might find themselves nailed immovably to a Roman cross—a torture device so horrific that it was reserved for the vilest of criminals, and one that was never to be discussed in public or polite speech. The cross was an ever-present reminder of the evil age.

Many Jewish people of that day, because of this ongoing suffering, did not place their hope in "the present age" but looked forward to an "age to come." In this future age, God would make things right. God would raise up the faithful who had long since passed away, and his goodness would rule the day. It would be an age when God wipes away all tears from his people's eyes.

But Jews in this time knew that was not the day they lived in. They had stories that said otherwise. For example, a story found in 2 Maccabees takes place more than a century and a half before Jesus and tells of a time of great persecution. A tyrant named Antiochus Epiphanes had taken control of the land of Israel and made it illegal for the Jewish people to practice their faith. Circumcision was outlawed. Synagogues were destroyed. Torah scrolls burned. Even worse, an altar to Zeus was set up in the Holy of Holies, and pigs were sacrificed there. (The Holy of Holies being the most sacred place on earth to the Jewish people and pigs being an unclean animal in Jewish law made this act especially profane.) Resisting Antiochus would lead to torture and death.

In this time, the book of 2 Maccabees tells the story of a mother and her seven sons. The account is horrific, but it's important that we take a quick look at it.

> It happened also that seven brothers and their mother were arrested and were being compelled by the king, under torture with whips and thongs, to partake of unlawful pig's flesh. One of them, acting as their spokesman, said, "What do you intend to ask and learn from us? For we are ready to die rather than

transgress the laws of our ancestors." The king fell into a rage and gave orders to have pans and caldrons heated. These were heated immediately, and he commanded that the tongue of their spokesman be cut out and that they scalp him and cut off his hands and feet, while the rest of the brothers and the mother looked on. When he was utterly helpless, the king ordered them to take him to the fire, still breathing, and to fry him in a pan. (2 Maccabees 7:1-5 NRSVUE)

Brutal, I know.

And if this story is not bad enough, it gets worse. One by one, every brother is tortured and killed in a horrific manner. But I want us to pay close attention to what the brothers say as they face torture and death. In his sufferings another brother speaks: "And when he was at his last breath, he said, 'You accursed wretch, you dismiss us from this present life, but the King of the universe will raise us up to a renewal of everlasting life, because we have died for his laws.'" (2 Maccabees 7:9 NRSVUE).

The King will raise us up.

This is incredibly important. If ever there was a moment to doubt the goodness of God or wrestle with that age-old question about how a good God could exist with so much evil in the world, it was at that moment. The evil tyrant is killing every family member one by one and in the most horrific of ways! Nevertheless, what does the brother proclaim? He says, "Yes, we are going to die, but that is not the end; God will raise us up." In other words, he presupposed that this world was filled with evil and suffering, but he also presupposed there would come a day when the innocent would be vindicated. The king would raise him up.

The brothers are tortured and killed one by one, in order of age. Before he dies, another brother speaks: "One cannot but choose to die at the hands of mortals and to cherish the hope God gives of being raised again by him. But for you there will be no resurrection to life!" (2 Maccabees 7:14 NRSVUE).

The horror keeps going. Another brother has his hands chopped off but trusts that what he lost, he will receive again in the age to come.

Directly to the tyrant another brother says, "But do not think that you will go unpunished for having tried to fight against God!" (2 Maccabees 7:19 NRSVUE).

After six of the seven brothers have been killed, the mother speaks these words to her one remaining son:

> I do not know how you came into being in my womb. It was not I who gave you life and breath nor I who set in order the elements within each of you. Therefore the Creator of the world, who shaped the beginning of humankind and devised the origin of all things, in his mercy gives life and breath back to you again, since you now forget yourselves for the sake of his laws. . . . Do not fear this butcher but prove worthy of your brothers. Accept death, so that in God's mercy I may get you back again along with your brothers. (2 Maccabees 7:22-23, 29 NRSVUE)

Gut-wrenching, I know. So why do I share this story with you? Because this story, written down by Jews about one hundred years before Jesus, was meant to encourage others in faithfulness to God. It reminded them not only of *where* they were, but of *when* they were.

They were in the olam hazeh, the present age. An age filled with pain and suffering and injustice. The faithful were not to be shocked when tyrants emerged; they were to presuppose them. This world was filled with madmen, demons, and tribulation, but the faithful were to cling to the hope that God would make things right. He would raise them up, and the words of the prophets would ring true: justice would flow like a river, and the glory of God would flood the earth. Yes, it's dark and the night is long . . . but the sun will rise.

For the faithful living in the time of the Maccabees, their feet were planted in the present, but their eyes were fixed on the future.

BREAD AND WINE

At the heart of Christian practice is a ritual that began on the night Jesus was betrayed. This ritual has two main elements: bread and wine.[1] On that night, Jesus gathered his disciples and said of the bread, "This is my body, which is given for you" (Luke 22:19). Of the wine he said, "This is my blood of the covenant" (Matthew 26:28). The disciples then partook of the bread and partook of the cup. For more than two thousand years, Christians have repeated this act.

This ritual, which is also a sacrament, goes by many different names depending on which tradition is speaking about it. It is known as the Eucharist, Communion, the Lord's Table, the Lord's Supper, and more.

In a letter written by the apostle Paul, he reminds the young Christian community in Corinth of the words that Jesus gave when he hosted the first Communion meal, and Paul also offers some additional information. For the bread Paul says, "For I received from the Lord what I also delivered to you, that the Lord Jesus on the night when he was betrayed took bread, and when he had given thanks, he broke it, and said, 'This is my body, which is for you. *Do this in remembrance of me*'" (1 Corinthians 11:23-24, italics added).

For the cup he says, "In the same way also he took the cup, after supper, saying, 'This cup is the new covenant in my blood. Do this, as often as you drink it, in remembrance of me.' For as often as you eat this bread and drink the cup, *you proclaim the Lord's death until he comes*" (1 Corinthians 11:25-26, italics added).

This is easy to miss, but every time we take Communion, the words of Paul tell us we are pulled in two directions. The bread tells us to look back to the *past* and remember. The cup speaks of a new covenant that the follower of Christ is *presently* now a part of. Both the bread and the cup, when taken together, then proclaim the Lord's death until a *future* event occurs—namely, his return. In other words, you exist in the present, yes, but you also have one foot in the past: *take this and remember*. And you also have one foot in the future: *proclaim the Lord's death until he comes*.

We look back to the past, but we also simultaneously look to the future. We remember the death of Christ but also anticipate his return. Our bodies occupy the present space, firmly established in the new covenant, but our hearts and minds see in two directions. Communion is a past-present-future activity.

But why is this important, and what in the world does it have to do with the brutal story of the mother and the seven sons? Knowing the past, present, and future will help us to know exactly when in the story we are and how to live faithfully in that *when*. Communion functions, among many other things, as a GPS system in which we triangulate our coordinates. But the GPS is not of location, but of time.

We exist in the *present*, an evil age filled with hardship and suffering. But we remember what Christ did in the *past*, which guarantees what will happen in the *future*: the return and end of all evil and suffering. In Communion, the past and the future come together in the present. We see the beginning, middle, and end of the story. Christ behind me, Christ with me, Christ before me.[2]

What is it then from the past, present, and future that is important for us to know? First, let's deal with the past. At the center of the Christian claim is the idea that God himself went into death itself, and not any old death, but the worst type of death—death on a cross.

The story of Jesus is a story of extremes. It takes you from one end of reality to the other. Christ is God; therefore, there is nothing higher than him. There is nothing above him. He is the edge. He is the limit. Yet he goes to the lowest of lows. He comes down and takes upon himself the nature of humans. But he goes still further down. He does not just come as a human; he becomes a servant in our world. But that's still not far enough. He is the servant who comes to die. But it's not just any death that he endures; he dies a slave's death, in torture and agony, nailed to a Roman cross. From the highest of heavens to the hell of the cross, the story of Christ moves from one end to the other. There is no one who ever went so great a distance from high to low.

While you were an enemy of God, Christ died for you. You were bought with royal blood. When people say the gospel is the greatest story ever told, that's not just rhetoric; it really is the greatest story ever told. You can't conceive of a greater story. From the heights of which there is nothing higher to the depths of which there is nothing lower. From throne to cross. From crown of glory to crown of cursed ground. From heaven to grave. Christ does this for his people. What happened in the past changes everything.

"Take this and remember."

What does this past then say about the present? If you know that one of such worth did this for you, it will enable you to live differently in the present. It says that no matter what happens to you, no matter what has been done to you, or what you have done to others, you are loved.

Who do you belong to? You belong to him. Does he love you? Yes. Did he die for you? Yes. Christ says no one took his life from him; rather, he gave up his life freely. What should you think about yourself if one so good, true, and beautiful would freely go to the cross to save you?

You are known. He knows you better than you know yourself. He knows your name and he knows every hair on your head. He knows all the stuff that you wish you could bury and never let see the light of day, and yet he loves you.

Say it to yourself: *I am loved. Jesus loves me.* Even better, say it out loud: "I am loved. Jesus loves me."

What about the future?

This is the blood of the covenant, which you belong to. Christ's blood shed on your behalf. The innocent for the guilty. When we take Communion, we are pledging our allegiance to him by proclaiming his death and resurrection until he returns. The return of Christ is anticipated every time we take Communion. The King will return for his people.

The present time may be filled with hardship and suffering, but Communion tells us how the story will ultimately end. There will be a day when the current difficulties cease, when all crooked lines are made straight, when all dissonant notes are resolved. The long defeat will turn to everlasting victory.

With this perspective, you will not be surprised with suffering in this life; you will presuppose it. You will expect the Antiochuses of this world to rise, but you will also, like the mother and her seven sons, know that you will be raised in glory. You will know that every evil deed will meet the righteous judge. In the end, no one will get away with evil. Everyone will answer to God.

Knowing the future fuels faithfulness in the present.

The weapon of the tyrant is always the ruin of life. The tyrant comes to steal, kill, and destroy. Their greatest weapon is always the fear of death. But what happens when someone believes the sting of death has been removed? What happens when death only leads to life? When someone grasps this, they can begin to live with courage not normally found.

Countless times I have seen people shellshocked by the evil they see and encounter. It's as if their understanding of reality does not have the categories to properly process evil. In a materialist story, there can be no true evil. There might be mistakes, brokenness, misalignment, and dysfunction, but never evil in the purest sense. For the materialist, we are just machines—machines that may not be working right, but never image-bearers filled with diabolical intent.

Communion takes us back to the cross, the visible symbol of the worst of human evil (a torture device specifically crafted to inflict the worst possible pain on a human being). The Christian story centers on the most innocent of persons given over to the worst of evils. Therefore, Christians ought to orient themselves to presuppose this world is filled with hardship, suffering, and evil. If it happened to the Son of God, it can happen to us.

Christians are not surprised when great evil occurs. But here is the thing: we are also not surprised when great good occurs. We are not only not surprised, but rather we anticipate great good coming out of even the darkest places.

Why? Because if God can take a cross, a symbol of horror unimaginable, and turn that into an image of hope, then certainly we ought to expect the good to break through in the darkest of corners. If he can take the cross, an image so reviling that one dared not look at it, and make it the image that billions of people fix their eyes on to find peace, hope, and love, then surely he can make new whatever it is in your life that needs restoration.

The cross says of the past, no matter how bad it may be, God can turn it around.

We in the present look back to the cross and see an image transformed. Likewise, we look to the future for Christ to return and transform all of creation. Two thousand years ago Christ put a stake in the ground—a cross—and laid claim to our world, and he will return to make all things new.

JUST A SYMBOL

How, then, should we act when we take Communion? What are we to think is occurring when we take this sacred meal? Well, unfortunately, there is a ton of debate around that question. People have been fighting about it for a very long time. Some traditions say the bread and wine turn into the actual body and blood of Jesus, while some on the other end say Communion is a memorial service that simply remembers what Christ did.

I am in no way going to try and settle the debate here (although I do have my opinions). What I would like to do is point us in a direction that Scripture is clear about and offer something that at minimum all Christians should agree on. This direction has less to do with "what" we believe is happening (which is still very important) and more to do with "how" we behave when it happens. My concern is with how we act.

Listen to what the apostle Paul tells the Christians in Corinth: "Whoever, therefore, eats the bread or drinks the cup of the Lord in an unworthy manner will be guilty concerning the body and blood of the Lord" (1 Corinthians 11:27).

This is easy to miss, but Paul is making it clear that when we act in an unworthy manner toward the bread and the cup, it is not the bread and cup we are acting against; we are acting against the body and blood of our Lord. The guilt incurred is not concerning the bread and wine but rather the body and blood.

Often, in many church traditions, when Communion is taken, the emphasis will be on the elements being "just a symbol." The word "just" is often emphasized to make sure no one for even a second thinks anything more than just symbolism is taking place.

But consider this: when symbolism is properly understood, it never diminishes the weight of what is occurring. In fact, the symbol is meant to stand in place of the reality so that we act as if the symbol is the reality that it is pointing to. In other words, if it's truly "just a symbol," then we ought not act like it's "just a symbol."

Confusing, I know. Let me explain.

Imagine a husband removing his wedding ring before a work trip to Vegas, and imagine his motives are not the best. In one sense, it's just a symbol, so no big deal, right? But a wife would never look at her husband's actions and tell herself, *It's just a symbol, so no big deal.* Rather, she understands that the symbol stands in place of a greater reality—namely, their marriage. To remove the ring is to sin against the marriage.

Or imagine a group of protesters taking their country's flag and burning it in the streets. And imagine another group rushing forward in anger, attempting to stop their country's flag from burning and being treated with such disregard. Both parties, the group burning the flag and the group upset at the burning of the flag, understand what's going on. Neither party says, "No big deal, it's just a flag." No. They know the flag is standing in place of something—namely, the country's people, values, culture, and ideals. They both agree on that. One side, however, is protesting those things, and the other side wants to affirm those things. But neither one believes that this act of protest is meaningless.

So, no matter your view on Communion, even if you believe it's "just a symbol," you act in a manner as if you are approaching what the symbol is standing in place of. This is exactly how Paul instructs us to behave. He warns us that if we sin against the bread and cup, we sin against what they stand in place of: the body and blood of our Lord.

This means whenever Communion takes place, we ought to behave in a manner worthy of what the elements stand in place of. In a materialist world, time and space are always focused on things below, earthly things trying to be given heavenly weight. We pursue cheap rituals that are impostors standing in place of the rituals that bring together things above with things below. In the midst of a materialist culture, the church has a ritual, a ritual in which we enter into true sacred space and sacred time. We see the bread and the cup, and we know what they mean. Their material reality points to a greater reality.

Let's go back to the ritual of baptism for a moment. Baptism is like a wedding, when we first pledge our love, loyalty, commitments, and allegiance to our spouse. In baptism we declare to Christ and before witnesses that Christ is our highest love.

Communion is the wedding ring of the new covenant. As often as you take Communion, you experience an anniversary in which you repledge your love, loyalty, commitments, and allegiance to Christ. We remember the cross that brought about the covenant, we confess our loyalty in the present, and we declare our ongoing faithfulness till death (or until he returns). In Communion we pledge again to keep wearing the wedding ring. We pledge ourselves to the original promises made.

All of this means Communion is no small endeavor. When we take it, our posture should change. Our countenance should change. At the church I pastor, we stand when we take Communion. This is to signal to our bodies that the King is in our midst. He is here with his people. Stand up straight. Wipe the sleep from your eyes. The Son of God is before you.

PLEASE STAND FOR THE PLEDGE OF ALLEGIANCE

When I was in grade school, we started every morning with the Pledge of Allegiance. We stood, faced the flag, and repeated the same words every morning. It is important to regularly pledge allegiance to Jesus. Communion is an invitation to do this regularly and consistently. Church traditions vary on how often Communion is done. My church does it weekly. It's good to pledge allegiance frequently. It's good to remind yourself what time it is. It's good to remind yourself of what Christ did on your behalf. It's good to remind yourself of what is coming in the future.

When the King is before us, we pledge allegiance in the present, remembering the past, and looking forward to the future. We presuppose this world is filled with evil. But we live faithfully in the present, fueled and empowered by the past event of the cross, and then we wait patiently with expectation for the King to return. Telos exists even in a world filled with trials. In Communion we behold the entire story: past, present, future.

Whenever you take Communion, reaffirm your commitment to him. You were made to serve him. Pledge again your allegiance like you did at baptism. Triangulate your position: past, present, and future. Act as if this two-thousand-year-old ritual has the power to sustain you in evil times . . . because it does.

Christ behind me,
Christ with me,
Christ before me.

12

Thanksgiving

PEOPLE OF FAITH WILL OFTEN ASK, "How can I know God's will for my life?" This question can manifest itself in a number of ways. You might want to know what college to go to, what career path to choose, who you should marry, or any number of endless questions you seek answers to. So much anxiety, time, and worry are spent on one key question: *What is God's will for my life?*

Well, I want you to know something: I know the will of God for your life.

Yes, you. I know the will of God for your life.

That's right. I can tell you with absolute certainty.

Are you ready?

Brace yourself.

The will of God . . . for you . . . is to . . . *be thankful.*

I know that's a bit of a letdown, but it's true. And I know you might think that it's a simple answer, but if you truly understood what takes place when we give thanks, then you would know it has the power to transform your life. And this is not just me making up some self-help principle. This is something grounded in the Scriptures and something Christians have practiced for two thousand years.

Listen to the words of the apostle Paul: "*Give thanks* in all circumstances; for this is the *will of God* in Christ Jesus for you" (1 Thessalonians 5:18, italics added).

The will of God for your life is to *give thanks.*

Keep in mind who is saying this. This is not some pie-in-the-sky advice from someone who has lived a life of luxury and has no idea what hardship looks like. It's also not popcorn pop culture advice, like, "Just be more optimistic. Remember, the glass is half full, after all." Nor is this anything remotely similar to "the power of positive thinking."

Sometimes we are tempted to think we don't have much to give thanks for. Sometimes we look at the lives of others and say to ourselves, *If only I had their life, it would be easy to be thankful.* At this point Paul offers some words that we should pay attention to, because if anyone should have reason not to give thanks for the life they were given, it's him. Listen to just a sampling of the sufferings he endured, which he lists in the book of 2 Corinthians:

> Five times I received at the hands of the Jews the forty lashes less one. Three times I was beaten with rods. Once I was stoned. Three times I was shipwrecked; a night and a day I was adrift at sea; on frequent journeys, in danger from rivers, danger from robbers, danger from my own people, danger from Gentiles, danger in the city, danger in the wilderness, danger at sea, danger from false brothers; in toil and hardship, through many a sleepless night, in hunger and thirst, often without food, in cold and exposure. And, apart from other things, there is the daily pressure on me of my anxiety for all the churches. (2 Corinthians 11:24-28)

Paul is a man who gives thanks in *all* circumstances. In listing what he has suffered, Paul disarms our excuses. He was tortured multiple times, abandoned, betrayed, left for dead, falsely accused, and knew danger at every turn. Nevertheless, it is this same Paul who says it is the will of God in Christ to gives thanks.

Some might say, "Well, maybe he started off on the bright side, but I am sure by the end of his life he was a bitter old man." Not so. Look at Paul's words in the book of 2 Timothy. This is the last letter Paul wrote, when he was at the end of his life and facing execution.

He would soon be killed for proclaiming the very Jesus he had spent his life giving thanks to. What was his attitude in that moment? What was his thanksgiving like as the shadow of death lurked over his head? Listen to how he begins this final letter.

> Paul, an apostle of Christ Jesus by the will of God according to the promise of the life that is in Christ Jesus,
>
> To Timothy, my beloved child:
>
> Grace, mercy, and peace from God the Father and Christ Jesus our Lord.
>
> *I thank God* whom I serve, as did my ancestors, with a clear conscience, as I remember you constantly in my prayers night and day. (2 Timothy 1:1-3, italics added)

Paul is proclaiming grace, mercy, and peace. In the midst of approaching death, he clings to the promise of life. And one of the first things he mentions in this letter is that he gives thanks to God. Paul had learned that he had reason to give thanks independent of earthly circumstances. No matter what was happening down here below, there was a greater reality that determined his true lot. Even though death was the sentence below, he looked up to his God and knew of a promise of life.

Most importantly, there was a truth he deeply held, a truth that was such unbelievably good news that no matter what had befallen him he still had reason to rejoice. What was this truth? It was what Jesus his Messiah had done for him.

"And the life I now live in the flesh I live by faith in the Son of God, who loved me and gave himself for me" (Galatians 2:20).

A GOOD NEWS PEOPLE

The first Christians went around the Roman Empire declaring good news, the good news of what Jesus had done: his life, his death, and his resurrection. The idea that the Creator of all things loves humanity and died for them was a life-changing and history-altering claim.

Even more so, this love was so strong that the first Christians believed there was nothing that could separate them from it. No matter what happened, the love of God would hold them. Paul boldly and triumphantly declared, "I am sure that neither death nor life, nor angels nor rulers, nor things present nor things to come, nor powers, nor height nor depth, nor anything else in all creation, will be able to separate us from the love of God in Christ Jesus our Lord" (Romans 8:38-39).

So, like Paul, even in suffering the first Christians believed they always had reason to give thanks. The first Christians were a good news people. They were able to say, "Christ loves us and gave himself for us," therefore:

"We are forever and always a good news people."

"We can forever and always rejoice."

"We can forever and always give thanks."

Had a bad day? You still have good news. Lost your job? You still have good news. Got bad news from the doctor? You still have good news. Even if World War III breaks out and you are just moments away from the nukes being launched, you . . . still . . . have . . . good . . . news.

Jesus knows you, loves you, died for you, and gives you the promise of life.

The reason these transcendent truths are so important is that if your thankfulness is dependent on the ever-changing circumstances of this fallen and fickle world, then your level of thankfulness will always be a roller coaster ride. Your favorite sports team gets eliminated from the playoffs, you have a bad day at work, you get cut off on the freeway . . . there are a thousand reasons why you might not be in the mood to give thanks. This is why a grateful posture is rooted in that which is above.

Paul's reason for being thankful was that the Son of God loved him and gave himself for him. This is not to say we are not to be thankful for things below. Quite the opposite. We are to give thanks for friends and family, and we are to give thanks for lesser things like food, good days, and vacations. But we recognize their source and remember the One from who all blessings flow.

This understanding is demonstrated by Jesus himself. Many times in Scripture we see Jesus give thanks before eating. John 6:11 records, "Jesus then took the loaves, and when he had *given thanks*, he distributed them to those who were seated" (italics added).

It should be obvious that Jesus is directing his thanks toward someone—namely, his father above. Jesus, in fact, might have recited a prayer similar to a prayer that Jewish people have been using for a very long time to give thanks for bread: *Barukh atah Adonai Elohenu melekh ha'olam hamotsi lekhem min ha'arets* which translated means "Blessed are you, LORD our God, King of the universe, who brings forth bread from the earth."

The prayer is short but loaded with insight. God is King. He provides bread. Therefore, we bless and give thanks to him. We experience the goodness of God above, here below, in bread along with a host of many other blessings. Thanksgiving thus becomes a regular and daily occurrence. We can give thanks *for* friends, family, spouse, work, food, shelter, the air in our lungs . . . but we must give thanks *to* someone for these things. Thankfulness for these things must ultimately be directed at their source, our Father above.

EMBODIED THANKS

There is a critical component to giving thanks that has been lost in the modern world and is right in line with everything we have talked about so far. Thanksgiving is something that should be embodied. We don't just think thankful thoughts; we express our thanks with our bodies.

We are to give thanks out loud.

We are to sing songs of thanksgiving.

We are to sit around a meal and eat and give prayers of thanksgiving.

We are to change our physical posture when we pray.

Try this: begin your morning by giving thanks. Wake up; breathe in. Acknowledge that this breath is a gift. You were not guaranteed to wake up. Feel your chest rise and fall as you slowly inhale and exhale. Your body has the spirit of life in you. Do not pick up your phone; set your first thoughts on ones of thanksgiving. Bring all that you are grateful for to the center of your attention. List them before your heavenly Father.

Get out of bed. Get down on your knees as if kneeling before a king, because you are. Let your body respond to ultimate truth. God is before you. Speak to him and tell him you are ready to serve him this day. It is a gift, honor, and privilege to serve him. Remind yourself that he loves you and that his Son died for you.

Try starting your day like this for a few weeks and see what happens.

A DIRECTION TO PRAY

You might ask yourself, *Why is it so important for me to do all this stuff with my body?* Even asking this question reveals how far we have come from the traditions of the faith. Our ancestors in the faith simply assumed that the body makes a difference.

The apostle James was called "Old Camel Knees" because it was said he had callouses on his knees from kneeling in prayer so often. When the prophet Daniel heard prayer was made illegal, "he went to his house where he had windows in his upper chamber open toward Jerusalem. He got down on his knees three times a day and prayed and gave thanks before his God, as he had done previously" (Daniel 6:10). Many Jewish prayers are given facing Jerusalem to this day, and many Jewish families place a plaque called a *mizrah* (meaning "east" in Hebrew) on a wall in their home to mark the direction they are to face when praying.

Likewise, many Christians have historically faced the east to pray. This was done for many reasons. Christ was said to return from the east (Matthew 24:27). Jesus was the "dawn that enlightened the world."[1] Christians throughout history would also fix crosses on walls facing the east to remind themselves of the direction of the Garden of Eden. The church father Basil the Great assumed everyone knew the tradition of praying to the east.[2] Praying in the direction of Christ's return anticipates the climax of earth's story.

Bowing to pray, set times to pray, directions to face and pray . . . the practice and habits of prayer are ritualized in time, space, and the body.

At some point you might have heard something like, "You can just pray in your heart." I want to be clear that there is nothing wrong with a silent prayer done in the heart. But prayer can also have other dimensions. Prayers of thanks should not remain only on the inside; they are meant to manifest themselves in the world, to be seen and heard by your ears and others'.

GOD IS GOOD

Similar to the apostle Paul, there is another story in which someone might have had reason not to give thanks. The man was completely innocent; he had never done anything wrong to anyone. He lived his life caring, loving, and serving. He fed the poor, welcomed the outcast, and healed the sick.

Nevertheless, in his early thirties the tides of popular opinion turned against him. He was betrayed, arrested, tortured, and crucified. Even more startling is the fact that this man knew it was all going to happen. He told his followers that the religious establishment would hand him over to be killed. He told his followers that even they—his own followers—would abandon him and scatter like sheep without a shepherd. He even warned one of his closest disciples that he would deny him.

Before Jesus went to the cross, he shared a meal with the ones he called friends. At the end of this meal, the Scriptures record something fascinating that is easily glossed over and missed by many readers. The Bible tells us that before Jesus went to the cross, he sang a song with his friends.

"And when they had sung a hymn, they went out to the Mount of Olives" (Matthew 26:30).

Wouldn't it be incredible to know what song Jesus sang? I mean, wouldn't this song be one of the most important songs in history? What were the words sung by Jesus moments before he was handed over to be crucified? Were the lyrics filled with fear of what's to come? Were the lyrics questioning his Father and his goodness? Were they lyrics full of anger toward his enemies?

No. They were nothing like that.

What if I told you they were words of thanksgiving? What if I told you he defied the evil and ugliness of this world by speaking of the goodness of his Father before horror befell him?

The book of Psalms was the hymnbook for Ancient Israel. These were the words that were sung over and over again. Within the book there is a collection of psalms that were used during Passover. These psalms are called the Hallel Psalms and consist of Psalms 113–118. Traditionally, Psalm 118 was sung as the last song after the Passover meal. This tradition is old, going back to the time of Jesus. And although we are not absolutely certain because the Scripture is not specific, we have good reason to think that the last song Jesus sang on Passover night was Psalm 118.

Before you rush ahead and see what Psalm 118 says, I want you to pause and remember the details of the story.

Jesus has shared a meal with his friends. He has washed the feet of those who would betray, deny, and abandon him. He has taught, forgiven, and healed the people of Israel. He first entered Jerusalem with chants of "Hosanna", but soon those chants will change to "Crucify him!" He will be beaten and battered and nailed to a Roman cross. In nakedness he will suffer a death so horrific that Rome never dared kill their own citizens in such a manner. As he hangs in agony, he will be mocked and derided. There, suspended between heaven and earth, Jesus will writhe in agony for hours. There he will die between two thieves.

Imagine now, what words would you sing moments before this is all set in motion? What thoughts would occupy your mind? What words would you expect to be on the lips of anyone sentenced to such doom as was just described?

Jesus sings Psalm 118. This is how it begins:

"Oh give thanks to the Lord, for he is good; for his steadfast love endures forever!"

Take it in. When darkness falls and the light of day is nowhere to be found . . . give thanks to the Lord, for he is good.

Below are the words of Psalm 118 in their entirety. I know it's easy to rush through long quotes, but trust me, read these verses slowly and intently—it's worth it. As you read them, picture Christ going to the cross. The words are prophetic and haunting, yet hopeful and triumphant.

> Oh give thanks to the Lord, for he is good;
>   for his steadfast love endures forever!
> Let Israel say,
>   "His steadfast love endures forever."
> Let the house of Aaron say,
>   "His steadfast love endures forever."
> Let those who fear the Lord say,
>   "His steadfast love endures forever."
> Out of my distress I called on the Lord;
>   the Lord answered me and set me free.
> The Lord is on my side; I will not fear.
>   What can man do to me?
> The Lord is on my side as my helper;
>   I shall look in triumph on those who hate me.
> It is better to take refuge in the Lord
>   than to trust in man.

> It is better to take refuge in the Lord
>   than to trust in princes.
> All nations surrounded me;
>   in the name of the Lord I cut them off!
> They surrounded me, surrounded me on every side;
>   in the name of the Lord I cut them off!
> They surrounded me like bees;
>   they went out like a fire among thorns;
>   in the name of the Lord I cut them off!
> I was pushed hard, so that I was falling,
>   but the Lord helped me.
> The Lord is my strength and my song;
>   he has become my salvation.
> Glad songs of salvation
>   are in the tents of the righteous:
> "The right hand of the Lord does valiantly,
>   the right hand of the Lord exalts,
>   the right hand of the Lord does valiantly!"
> I shall not die, but I shall live,
>   and recount the deeds of the Lord.
> The Lord has disciplined me severely,
>   but he has not given me over to death.
> Open to me the gates of righteousness,
>   that I may enter through them
>   and give thanks to the Lord.
> This is the gate of the Lord;
>   the righteous shall enter through it.
> I thank you that you have answered me
>   and have become my salvation.
> The stone that the builders rejected
>   has become the cornerstone.
> This is the Lord's doing;
>   it is marvelous in our eyes.

This is the day that the LORD has made;
    let us rejoice and be glad in it.
Save us, we pray, O LORD!
    O LORD, we pray, give us success!
Blessed is he who comes in the name of the LORD!
    We bless you from the house of the LORD.
The LORD is God,
    and he has made his light to shine upon us.
Bind the festal sacrifice with cords,
    up to the horns of the altar!
You are my God, and I will give thanks to you;
    you are my God; I will extol you.
Oh give thanks to the LORD, for he is good;
    for his steadfast love endures forever! (Psalm 118:1-29)

If one as innocent as Jesus, condemned to die a death such as this, can still give thanks, certainly we can too.

UNGRATEFULNESS IS EASY

Have you ever noticed how easy it is to be ungrateful? How easy it is to complain, bicker, grumble, whine, point fingers, and want more than what we have been given? One of the greatest markers that will set you apart from the world is learning the sacred practice of thanksgiving. Paul the apostle, in writing a different letter to a different church, told them to "do all things without grumbling or disputing, that you may be blameless and innocent, children of God without blemish in the midst of a crooked and twisted generation, among whom you shine as lights in the world, holding fast to the word of life, so that in the day of Christ I may be proud that I did not run in vain or labor in vain" (Philippians 2:14-16).

What is fascinating is that in these verses Paul is describing what Christian living ought to look like and then comparing it to the "crooked and twisted generation." One of the key differences he lists is that Christians ought not be a grumbling people. In this, thanksgiving becomes our stand against an ungrateful world. To give thanks is to rebel against a world that says you always need more. To give thanks is to defy a world that says it's never enough. To give thanks is to counter the materialist story, to look up and see where goodness comes from. Your life has meaning, so turn and thank the Creator for it. To give thanks is to contrast yourself with the crooked and twisted generation in which you live.

Learn to give thanks. Make it a daily ritual. Set a time and change ordinary time to sacred time. Carve out a physical place and make it sacred space. Try putting a marker on a wall in your house facing the east to remind you from where your King will return. Wake up in the morning and thank God for everything good in your life. Are you married? Thank the Lord for your spouse. Do you have kids? Thank the Lord for your kids. Do you have food? Shelter? Clothes? Air in your lungs? Kneel before your King. Speak your words out loud. Let them resonate throughout your house. Make lists as long as possible for all the things you are thankful for.

And know this: even if this life has given you nothing but pain and heartache, even if no one has ever loved you or showed you a single act of kindness, even if you know this is the last day you will awake and that you will die alone, even if you will be betrayed, abandoned by friends, and led to a cross, give thanks. You still have reason to give thanks because Christ died for you. He loves you. He knows your name. You matter. Your life has meaning. You have a Father, and nothing in heaven, earth, or hell will ever separate you from his love.

Oh give thanks to the Lord, for he is good; for his steadfast love endures forever!

13

Bible

WE LIVE IN THE WRONG STORY.

We were told the universe is flat. Black and white. No color. We were made to believe that our five senses are the only detectors of reality. We were educated by institutions that said angels, demons, and spiritual powers belong to a world that died a long time ago.

We were told, "Humans know better now."

But still, something haunts us from the other side.

Imagine a children's adventure book where the poor peasant kid who labors on a farm finds out that he is secretly of royal blood. You know that type of story, right? Where the child is hidden away when the evil, dark lord kills his mother and father, but the faithful knight hides the boy away as the castle burns. Just as the child in a story like this grows and must find his identity, we, too, must rediscover our true story.

Think about how many stories make the revealing of a character's lost identity a critical plot point. Picture Luke Skywalker hanging from the Death Star above endless empty space below, and Darth Vader's voice saying, "I am your father." Or what about Simba in *The Lion King* looking into a small pond and hearing his father, Mufasa, say, "Remember who you are." These types of themes are repeated in our best stories. The discovery of one's true origin story radically reorients the character. It changes the way he views the world, his people, and maybe most importantly, himself. The hidden true story changes everything.

Just like these characters, we've been raised to believe the wrong story.

THE AIR OF EPHESUS

In chapter two we imagined ourselves living in the ancient city of Ephesus. Let's return there and recall the details. In the first century, Ephesus was located in a region called Asia Minor, near the eastern edge of the Roman Empire. If you lived there, everything in your community reinforced the story the culture was telling you. This was a story that said the gods and goddesses ruled the day. The stories of the gods and goddesses were retold in holidays, theater, architecture, and everything else that made the city, the city.

In Ephesus, there was a massive temple dedicated to the goddess Artemis. It was one of the Seven Wonders of the Ancient World. No matter where you stood in Ephesus, its structure imposed itself on you; you could not escape it. The temple sat on an elevated plateau so it could loom over the city. Its height then extended further with one hundred and twenty-seven columns, each sixty feet in height.[1] Artemis, with her story and architecture, was an ever-present reality to every person living in that city.

Now imagine yourself as a new Christian in that city. How powerless would you feel when everything around you told her story? What does that crucified Jewish man from Nazareth who died the slave's death have to say here? What power does he hold? What works of art have been dedicated to him? What cities have been founded on his name? What empires has he raised? No, that man has no place here. His story is swallowed up by the others.

In Ephesus, you live inside the story of the city, and whether you like it or not, if you take a stroll down the streets of Ephesus, you breathe the air its story gives you.

How can you possibly live faithfully as a Christian in that culture? You need a different story.

You need a better story.

A STORY TO LIVE INSIDE

Many Christians have spent a lot of time defending the Bible as the Word of God. This is incredibly important and a worthwhile endeavor, but sometimes we get so focused on defending the Bible that we forget to let its story *create the world we live in*.

As discussed at the beginning of this book, in any given culture, there is a dominant story. What most people do not realize is that this dominant story is not just a story you believe; it is, by default, the story you inhabit. You live inside the reality it creates.

Dominant stories have a way of putting a spell on us. Like a fairy tale where a sorcerer uses magic to stop the prince from having eyes to see the beauty of the peasant girl, we, too, see the world through spelled eyes.

For a Christian, the Bible provides the true story of reality. It gives us the story that we must inhabit. We must learn to live in the reality it creates. Reading Scripture thus invites us to see the world as it truly is. Scripture breaks the spell of materialism and properly orients our eyes.

Caution is needed at this point because it is possible to read the Bible while still having a spell over our eyes. This leads to a sort of materialist version of the Bible. However, when the Bible is read with a commitment to trust where it leads, little by little the spell is weakened, and we begin to see the world clearly.

One thousand years ago in Christian Europe, faith in Christ was reinforced at every level. Just as in Ephesus two millennia ago with Artemis, entire cities strengthened the dominant religious structure. The buildings were constructed with Christ in mind, the songs were written for Christ, the church was the center point of the city, and it was assumed that everyone would be baptized as a Christian. The default dominant story of the people in this environment was thoroughly Christian. In other words, it was really easy to have faith in Christ in that type of environment. It was so easy that Christianity was almost presupposed.

Now, I am not saying that genuine faith and love of Christ was just automatically given to everyone who lived in this type of world, but I am saying that the intellectual barriers to faith were nowhere near as strong as they are today. The lie the modern world believes is that we moved past religion because of scientific discovery and the fact that we are obviously so much smarter now than people were then. Many of us today often look back at our ancestors and see them as dumb and unenlightened. We are quick to assume that we live in an age without blind spots; we arrogantly think we have most things figured out.

At this point, it is important to remember the quote from C. S. Lewis from chapter two. He reminds us of what is true about our present age. He writes, "Our own age is also 'a period,' and certainly has, like all periods, its own characteristic illusions. They are likeliest to lurk in those widespread assumptions which are so ingrained in the age that no one dares to attack or feels it necessary to defend them."[2] The truth is, materialism is the new dominant story, and similar to the people living in Europe with its dominant Christian story one thousand years ago, we just presuppose its foundations.

A pagan three thousand years ago living in Egypt might look at the sun and see a representation of Amun-Ra, the sun god. A Christin living in France one thousand years ago might see the handiwork of God and the beauty of his creation in that same sun. And an atheist in twenty-first-century America might simply see a ball of gas burning at an extremely high temperature. The sun is always viewed through the story we inhabit.

This means the need for Scripture reading is of utmost importance in our current culture. Our culture is not building a society that reinforces Christian beliefs. At best, we say we are neutral toward religion, even though the belief in a neutral position toward religion makes sense only in our new materialist story.

In a world where materialism is the dominant story and is reinforced at every level of the culture, we must, like our ancestors in the faith, cling to the Bible. They, living in a world that maintained belief in countless gods and goddesses, held firmly to the biblical truth that there was indeed one true Lord of all. Likewise, we who live on the opposite end of the spectrum, amid a world that declares all gods and goddesses extinct, must cling to the biblical truth that there is indeed one true Lord over all.

The Bible invites its reader to experience the world as it truly operates. Yes, at first, the spell of materialism will influence your reading of the Bible. But take heart, you are not alone when you encounter the sacred words of this sacred book. This is God's book, and his Spirit works through this book. Slowly but surely, if you trust this book and allow it to lead you, it will break the power of cheap spells.

Moreover, you also have his church and two thousand years of her people who have also been led by his Spirit to read, digest, and teach its sacred truth. Their collective wisdom is always before us. People of every generation, from every tribe, tongue, and nation, are there to help us along the way.

It is important to remember that when you encounter the Scriptures, you do not encounter mere words. It is not just a book of collected documents. The Bible is of human and divine origin. God's words told through human authors. When you read the Bible, you encounter the God who it speaks of.

A SACRED CLOSET

As the men took their axes and broke every item in the synagogue, they went before a closet of sorts. This closet is referred to in Hebrew as the *Aron Haqodesh*, the Holy Ark. Inside the wooden closest was sacred space. It was where the Torah scrolls were kept. Normally this closet and what was housed inside were treated with the utmost care, protection, and reverence. But the men that day did not recognize whose words were written on these sacred scrolls. To them, the closet was mere wood, a piece of furniture crafted by the hands of men. Nothing more.

On a normal day this closet would not be harmed, but this was not a normal day. This was *Kristallnacht*—Night of Broken Glass. On this day, over one thousand synagogues would burn throughout Germany.

Before the closets were broken and burned, the soldiers would see something written on many of these closets. They would see these Hebrew words: דע לפני מי אתה עומד—*Da lifne mi attah omed*. In English: *Know Before Whom You Stand*.

For those who believed in these sacred Scriptures, their contents were from above. The Word of God written on material objects. A place for humanity to stand before the Almighty. But for horizontal humans, humans who believe there is nothing above the sun, their content is material to burn. It did not matter what was written on the closet. To the soldiers that night, it was nothing sacred. So often, humans are blind to the sacred in our midst. So, the axes came down and the closets were burned. They did not have eyes to see.

For our ancestors in the faith, the Bible was a lamp unto their feet and a light unto their path. It illuminated a dark world. The light it brought revealed how the world truly operates.

One person might see a ball of gas.

Another might see the beauty of God's creation.

One might see scrolls to be burned.

Another might see the very Word of God.

DROWNING IN A SEA OF STORIES

Think about how many stories we hear in a ten-year period. How many movies and TV shows do we watch? How many books do we read? How many narratives are given by the media? We are saturated in countless stories.

Imagine a world without the printing press, where there are only hand copies from handwritten original sources. Imagine a world where your sacred book is the central book of your culture. There is only one copy, and it is housed in your community's house of faith. This book gives your community most of the stories it tells. There is no Marvel Cinematic Universe. No *Star Wars*. No world of DC. There is only the universe created by this book.

You grow up hearing stories of David and Goliath, the three faithful boys in the fiery furnace, the great flood, and more. More than that, these are not just stories in a fictional universe, they are true stories; they are the stories of your people. Your people are a people of the book. The book is the story of your people—your ancestors—and the source that shapes your understanding of reality. Thus, not only do you encounter these stories in this book, but also you are a part of the grand story it is telling. This book's story is your story as well.

There is also something even more powerful about these stories that sets them apart from everything else. They are not just true stories; they are *more than true stories*. Normally, if we are reading a nonfiction account of something that happened in the past, we refer to it as a true story, but something more profound is going on with the Bible. The stories of the Bible reveal the fundamental nature of reality. In other words, they are not simply true because they happened in history; they are true because they are *always happening.* They explain something about the past, but they are also explaining the present.

Sallustius, a fourth-century historian, wrote this concerning myths: "These things never happened but always are."[3] Although this was written more than sixteen hundred years ago, many people are attracted to this definition of myth as something that can be applied to the Bible. It is common to hear a person say something like, "The stories of the Bible, of course, never actually happened, but they do contain lessons that might have value in them." Often, this is an attempt at a kind gesture given by the materialist to a believer as a polite way of saying, "Your stories aren't totally stupid."

To an unbelieving world, the Bible is filled with stories that probably did not happen and at best might contain some wisdom for the modern person. A believer, on the other hand, might focus on the stories of the Bible as historically and factually true. We might look at the archaeological evidence for a story like the fall of Jericho and use it to defend the Bible as historically reliable. This is a good and worthwhile endeavor, but often it does not go far enough. We stop at demonstrating the historical reliability and never articulate how the story is *still* happening. So, in some sense, both the believer and unbeliever in these two examples get something right, but also something wrong.

The Bible is not a book that contains myths; rather, it contains what we might call supra-myths. The stories of the Bible did not just happen, they are always happening.

This may be a bit confusing, so let's look at an example.

Let's go as far back into the past as we can go: the creation account at the very beginning of the Bible, in the book of Genesis. In our day, many people get stuck in the debate regarding the historical details of Adam, Eve, and the timing of the creation story. As important as those details are, if we focus too much on them, we can end up walking right past the gold in plain sight. Read the verse below and pay special attention to the English words in italics as well as the italicized Hebrew words in parentheses next to them.

"So when the woman *saw* (*ra'ah*) that the tree was *good* (*tov*) for food, and that it was a delight to the eyes, and that the tree was to be desired to make one wise, she *took* (*laqakh*) of its fruit and ate, and she also gave some to her husband who was with her, and he ate" (Genesis 3:6, Hebrew words in italics added).

In this verse, a pattern is established that is used throughout the Bible. Humans see (*ra'ah*) with the eyes that which is forbidden, declare it good (*tov*) in their own eyes, and then take (*laqakh*) what they should not.

In one sense, we learn about a historical event. The first humans see, declare the bad good, and take. But in another sense, something far more profound is occurring. This is not something that just happened, this is something that is always happening. And the Bible wants you to see it that way. Look for this pattern and you will find it all over the place:

See the forbidden, declare it good, then take it.

1. See
2. Good
3. Take

Here is an example:

It happened, late one afternoon, when David arose from his couch and was walking on the roof of the king's house, that he saw (*ra'ah*) from the roof a woman bathing; and the woman was very beautiful (*tov*). And David sent and inquired about the woman. And one said, "Is not this Bathsheba, the daughter of Eliam, the wife of Uriah the Hittite?" So David sent messengers and took (*laqakh*) her, and she came to him, and he lay with her. (2 Samuel 11:2-4, Hebrew words in italics added)

Bathsheba is forbidden to David; she is a married woman. Not even the king has license to take her. Nevertheless, David "sees" that she is "good" and "takes" her. Translations often create a bit of confusion here because they translate the Hebrew word *tov* as "beautiful." Translators render *tov* as "beautiful" in this context because the verse is referring to Bathsheba's physical appearance being good, that is, beautiful. So although "beautiful" is not a terrible translation, it does obscure the pattern.

The Bible uses the see-good-take pattern to clue the reader into seeing grave sin in David's actions. He is doing the same thing that our first ancestor did. And we follow the same pattern today; we forsake God's will for our lives, define good and evil in our own eyes, and then selfishly take what should not be ours.

In the book of Joshua, a man named Achan takes from his defeated enemies spoils that were forbidden. Read carefully how the Bible records Achan's own confession of the deed: "When I saw (*ra'ah*) among the spoil a beautiful (*tov*) cloak from Shinar, and 200 shekels of silver, and a bar of gold weighing 50 shekels, then I coveted them and took (*laqakh*) them" (Joshua 7:21).

Do you see the pattern? Humans see the forbidden, they desire it and call it good, and then they take it. In each of these three cases there is a recording of a historical fact, but do not treat these stories as mere historical facts. They are telling us about ourselves.

Humans always desire to decide right and wrong in their own eyes. They always invent their own moral code over against God's. They always look at that which is forbidden by God and say "mine." This is not simply true of Adam and David and Achan, it's true of all of us. These stories are so true, they don't merely record something that *happened* . . . they tell us something that is always *happening*.

Yes, there was a Tower of Babel in the past (Genesis 11), but there are always towers of Babel being built. Yes, there was a historical tyrant named Nebuchadnezzar (Daniel 3), who threatened the innocent with a furnace of fire, but there are always tyrants trampling upon the faithful. There are always beasts and monsters rising from the sea (Revelation 13). There are always giants that need slaying (1 Samuel 17). There are always rich young rulers who can't live without their wealth (Mark 10). There are always women at the well in need of something more than water (John 4). The crowds chanted, "Crucify him!" on Good Friday (Matthew 27:22 NIV), but humanity as a whole has looked at God and chanted the same.

The Bible reveals the patterns of reality at every level. This means the world of the Bible is not just a distant world that we look at to learn about the past; the world of the Bible is the same world as ours. We inhabit the same world and inhabit the same story.

If you want to see our world today as clearly as possible, read the Bible.

The examples that we have discussed so far have all been horrible news for humanity. We build towers, take the unlawful, eat the forbidden fruit . . . but there is good news. The Bible also reveals what God has done in the past. And when we look at what God has done in the past, we are also looking at his unchanging character. We see how he always is.

We behold a God who searches for Adam and Eve in the Garden, a God who pursues sinners. Humanity runs, hides, spills innocent blood, even curses the God who gives us our being, but God does not abandon us. The Scriptures demonstrate the never-changing love of a good Father. The Scriptures are the antidote to the materialist venom in our veins.

This world is filled with lies, and those lies come to us from many different directions. Sometimes they come from culture. Sometimes they come from loved ones. We even tell ourselves lies. But Scripture is the sword that cuts between truth and falsehood. It tells us the truth about ourselves, about God, and about everything in between. It tells us not only how the world ought to be but also how the world actually is. Wherever we find ourselves, Scripture counters the fabricated dominant story that would have us live within the confines of its prison walls. It tells the materialist that there is something beyond the walls. It tells us that there is a world beyond the boundaries of materialism. There is a world of good and evil, angels and demons, meaning and purpose . . . and a God who is our Father. There is wind and sun and life beyond the walls. Open the door of the prison cell, allow yourself to hear the wisdom of the Scriptures, and commit yourself to trusting the Bible, wherever it may lead.

This is exactly what our ancestors in the faith did. They were people of the book. The first Christians looked out at a world where the dominant story was one of paganism, full of gods and goddesses. It was a story that said there is no way a crucified man from northern Galilee who died a slave's death on a Roman cross could indeed be the one true King of kings. Nevertheless, in that world, they trusted the Word of God. They saw what all the Scriptures were pointing to, and they saw those Scriptures fulfilled in Jesus. They clung to the teachings of the apostles. They knew that this sacred book was telling them what they needed to know about the past, the present, the future, the world, themselves, and most importantly, God. They decided to live within that story. And within that story they found meaning.

The same must go for us today. We must live inside the story of Scripture. We should read it, memorize it, get into groups and read it out loud together. We should know what we have and who has given it to us. When you pick up a Bible:

דע לפני מי אתה עומד

Da lifne mi attah omed

Know before whom you stand.

This is his story. This is your story. This is our story.

14

Church

ALL YOU NEED IS A PERSONAL RELATIONSHIP with Jesus . . . well, sort of.

In order to unpack this, we are going to need to go all the way back to the beginning. Let's look at the story of the first humans in the first book of the Bible, Genesis. God creates Adam and puts him in a garden. This first human is also given a vocation. He is to tend the garden, and regarding that garden he is given a specific command: to "work it and keep it" (Genesis 2:15). At this point, sin has not entered the equation, and the first human exists in a garden paradise with God, animals, and the rest of creation. Nothing else needed, right? Wrong.

Even though Adam lives in a garden paradise with God, there is still something missing. How do we know this? Listen to what God says about the situation: "It is not good that the man should be alone" (Genesis 2:18). Wait, what? Alone? Adam is not alone. He has God, the animals, and the rest of creation to enjoy. But Adam is alone in another sense: Adam does not have anyone "like" him. He does not have another human. So, God creates another human from the side of Adam. This human is his counterpart. Her name is Eve, and when Adam sees her for the first time, Hebrew poetry flows from his lips. He declares:

> This at last is bone of my bones
> and flesh of my flesh;

she shall be called Woman,

because she was taken out of Man. (Genesis 2:23)

The Hebrew word for "man" is *iysh*, and the Hebrew word for "woman" is *iyshah*. Just like the English words *man* and *woman*, their pronunciations sound similar, yet they are different. Man/woman and iysh/iyshah. At the core of the first two humans is the reality that they are similar yet different. When Adam sees his iyshah, his words make it clear, that now, finally, there is one "like him." The animals were not flesh of his flesh or bone of his bone, but she is.

At the very beginning of the human story is this radical idea that we need the *other*. We need something that is like us but not us. Yes, all we need is God, but one of the ways God administers his goodness to humans is by giving them the *other*. We participate in the goodness of God above by receiving this gift below. Together, man and woman are given dominion over creation and given the task to reign over it in a way that reflects the goodness of God. The Bible goes on to say that this man and woman also become husband and wife, and that they "become one flesh" (Genesis 2:24).

One flesh. Unity in diversity. Oneness in a plurality. The beginning of the human story is one with a marriage scene. Two humans, different but alike, becoming one.

PLURAL AND SINGULAR

The apostle Paul wrote roughly half of the books in the New Testament. Guess how many times Paul uses the phrase "my Lord." Now guess how many times Paul uses the phrase "our Lord." Not a big difference in meaning between the two; one is singular, one is plural. But there is a big difference in usage. Here are the actual results:

My Lord = 1
Our Lord = 53

Pretty shocking. The first-person singular is worlds apart from the first-person plural. Is this simply a matter of grammatical preference? Or is there something much deeper going on? Do we see anything else in Paul that might help us get to the bottom of this? Listen to what Paul says to some of the very first Christians in the city of Ephesus:

"There is one body and one Spirit—just as you were called to the one hope that belongs to your call—one Lord, one faith, one baptism, one God and Father of all, who is over all and through all and in all" (Ephesians 4:4-6).

Obviously, there is a clear emphasis on the word *one*. And much of that makes sense—there is one God the Father, there is one Lord Jesus, and there is one Spirit. But one faith? One baptism? One body? How can that be? Clearly, there are millions of people who have their own faith, countless people who have different baptisms, a multitude of bodies that are Christian.

Paul would agree to this pushback, but he would also push forward. He would say that all those separate baptisms are part of the one baptism that the church administers. He would say we all have different individual accounts of putting our faith in Christ, but we all participate in the one true faith. And yes, we all have different bodies, but collectively we are the one body of Christ. There is a unity in our diversity, and a oneness in our plurality. Sound familiar?

Throughout his writings, Paul puts the utmost importance on the unity and oneness of the church. There are many examples of this, but here is one of my favorites: "So if there is any encouragement in Christ, any comfort from love, any participation in the Spirit, any affection and sympathy, complete my joy by being of the same mind, having the same love, being in full accord and of one mind" (Philippians 2:1-2).

Paul is in prison, and he says "complete my joy" by being unified. I don't know about you, but if I were stuck in a prison cell, my joy would rest on getting out of jail, not on the unity of some church miles away. Not for Paul though. The unity of this church was central. It was by no means some side mission; it was part of the heart of the mission for Paul.

Paul takes this lead from Christ himself. Look at what Jesus asks of his Father on the night when he is handed over and betrayed. Initially, Jesus prays specifically for his disciples, but then he goes on.

> I do not ask for these only, but also for those who will believe in me through their word, that they may all be *one*, just as you, Father, are in me, and I in you, that they also may be in us, so that the world may believe that you have sent me. The glory that you have given me I have given to them, that they may be *one* even as we are one, I in them and you in me, that they may become perfectly *one*, so that the world may know that you sent me and loved them even as you loved me. (John 17:20-23, italics added)

Jesus prays for his disciples, but then he also prays for all those who would come to believe based on their words. See the implication? Jesus prayed for you. Did you know that Jesus prayed for you on the night of his betrayal? Followers of Jesus alive today are, by extension, all those who believe because of the teaching of the apostles. And take note of what he prays for, that all believers would be *one*.

No one would have believed it on that night, but Jesus knew what he was going to build. He would build a church made of people from every tribe, tongue, and nation. He knew his church would expand and reach all people. And even though there are countless believers around the world, his prayer was that they would all be one. Jesus prayed for unity in the diversity. Just as a human body has trillions of living organisms that compose the whole, so the body of Christ is made of innumerable men, women, and children who compose his body.

There is one bride, one body, one church.

TENSION AND UNITY

The first Christians had to figure this unity thing out on the fly. Suddenly people were hearing the message of this crucified man from Nazareth, and their lives were being transformed. They immediately began to gather in small communities to receive the sacraments, hear the teaching of the Scriptures, pray, and worship together. You can imagine people from vastly different walks of life, all trying to come together and get along, yet being met with significant roadblocks.

Imagine a Roman solider sharing the bread and cup with a Jewish man sitting to his right. That Jewish man might have had a relative or friend crucified by a Roman solider. Imagine the rich now at the same level as the poor. Imagine a former prostitute and tax collector making small talk with a Pharisee who came to trust in Jesus. These differences obviously led to tension in the early church, so a lot of the New Testament is written to address these issues. But here's the point: even though it was an audacious goal, bringing together people from every tribe, tongue, and nation to form the one body, bride, and church of Christ was mission critical.

This one body was, of course, spread out in many cities and towns across the first-century world, but local gatherings were the embodied, localized expression of the one. Striving for unity in these small communities of faith was foundational. A divided body was something to fight against at all costs. As important as this is, it all presupposes something of incredible importance: striving for unity presupposes that you actually go to church.

RELATIONSHIP, NOT RELIGION

Somewhere right now there is a person hiking on a dirt trail through a beautiful forest. They have been walking for nearly four miles and are about to reach the summit. As they make it to the top they look out at the incredible view and see the glory of God's creation. They see the mountains, the trees, and a cloudless blue sky.

As they take it all in, they stretch out their arms and say, "This is my church."

No, no it's not.

Your hike might draw you closer to God. It might invoke a sense of awe before his creation. You might pray to him with greater appreciation for his creative might. But it is not church. Nature does not administer the sacraments to you. The mountains do not baptize. The trees do not read the Scriptures. The snack in your backpack is not Communion. The animals of the forest are not the gathering of the saints.

How could we think we could remove all these elements, isolate someone, and just because they are having a spiritual experience, equate that with what Christians for two thousand years have called "church"? Our culture's hyperindividualism is wreaking havoc on the gift of belonging and community. We have so emphasized a "personal relationship with Jesus" that we are forgetting to actually listen to the teachings of Jesus.

Or what about this: Have you ever heard someone say, "Christianity is not a religion, it's a relationship"? If you are like me, you have probably heard it countless times. And every time you hear it, it probably goes unchallenged and is received with nodding heads of approval. Maybe you have even said it with good intentions. But just stop and think about it—is that true? For sure, there is a relationship with God in Christianity, but does that exclude it from being a religion? How could a belief system with rites, rituals, sacred days, and a sacred book that teaches about sacred practices *not* be a religion? How in the world could "Christianity is not a religion" have become a beloved slogan?

Our individualism has led us to emphasize one component of the faith at the cost of the others. Yes, our faith entails a relationship with Jesus, but that's not all it is. Nowhere in the Bible does it even use the phrase "a personal relationship with Jesus." Nowhere in the

Bible does it say anything like, "You don't need to go to church, you just need a personal relationship with Jesus." Nowhere do we get a hint that the Bible would say, "Don't worry about all the rites, rituals, and religious stuff; the only thing that matters is your personal relationship with Jesus."

James the brother of Jesus helps us with a clarifying word.

"Religion that is pure and undefiled before God the Father is this: to visit orphans and widows in their affliction, and to keep oneself unstained from the world" (James 1:27).

Of course, Christianity is a religion. What James is doing is making a specific point about what kind of religion Christianity is. James is saying that it's not *only* about rite and ritual, but true religion must involve care for the orphan and the widow. He also says true religion is "to keep oneself unstained from the world." There is an ethical domain to the faith. Behavior matters. Christianity *is* a religion. It has rites, rituals, clergy, and behavioral commands. Here is the command not to forsake the local embodied gathering of believers:

"And let us consider how to stir up one another to love and good works, not neglecting to meet together, as is the habit of some, but encouraging one another, and all the more as you see the Day drawing near" (Hebrews 10:24-25).

Now, I know some of us might have heard the slogan "You don't go to church, you are the church." But is that slogan true? Well, again, sort of.

The Greek word that the New Testament uses for "the church" is *ekklēsia*. Ekklēsia literally refers to an assembly, a gathering of people. Church then, in one sense, is the individual believer, but church also is the gathering of those individual believers. It is not either or, it's both.

This understanding of both/and is woven throughout the New Testament. Probably the best way to illustrate the point is with a well-known verse, 1 Corinthians 6:19. Paul says, "Do you not know that your body is a temple of the Holy Spirit within you, whom you have from God?"

This is a well-quoted verse for good reason. The claim is hard to take in. You, with all your mistakes and faults, are the temple of the living God. The holy presence that was guarded for the entirety of the Old Testament now resides in you. You, as an individual, have the Spirit of God in you.

But there's more. Listen to Paul's words in 1 Corinthians 3:16: "Do you not know that *you* are God's temple and that God's Spirit dwells in you?" (italics added).

It sounds like Paul is saying the exact same thing here as he did in the previously quoted verse, but he's not. When Paul says in this verse that "you are God's temple," he does something incredibly important but completely obscured in English. In fact, it's nearly impossible to translate into English. In Greek, Paul uses a second-person plural. The problem is, in English we don't have an official second-person plural of "you." (Well, some of you do, because you grew up using a second-person plural of you: "y'all.") In 1 Corinthians 3:16, Paul says, "Y'all are the temple of God." Paul is saying that all believers now make up the temple of God.

Is this not a contradiction? Are individual believers the temple of God, or is it the collective whole of believers that make the temple? The answer is both. This language of being a "temple of God" is used of both individual believers and the church as a whole. Both realities are affirmed, but which one do you think receives all the emphasis in an individualistic culture? Yep, the singular. It's about *me*.

But what is a church without the *other*? How do you confess your sins to *one another*? How do you sing hymns and spiritual songs to *one another*? How do you bear *one another's* burdens? How do you comfort *one another*? How do you show hospitality to *one another*?[1]

And perhaps most importantly, how do we show the world we are one and thus demonstrate to the world that Christ was indeed sent by the Father if we do not regularly gather in sacred space and in sacred time?

There are roughly sixty "one another" commands in the New Testament. How do we do any of them without the other? These are the commands of Scripture; a professing Christian is called to obey them. In what sense can we say we are practicing Christianity without the other? In what sense can one even claim to be a Christian without the other? How could one possibly grow in faith without the other?

Indeed, it is not good for man to be alone.

A HELL ON EARTH

During the Vietnam War, many American POWs were taken to the Hỏa Lò Prison. There they experienced horrific treatment. Prisoners were often starved and tortured. The prison was sarcastically given the name the "Hanoi Hilton." One of the worst forms of torture practiced at the prison was solitary confinement. Prisoners were often kept completely isolated and not allowed to talk with another human being.

Solitary confinement can take you to the brink, to the edge of your sanity and the end of hope. Despair often sets in, and whatever remaining motivation to keep going fades. In this hell of a prison, the POWs found a way to maintain their humanity and thus found a way to hold on to hope and encourage one another. Without the ability to speak to one another, they began using a system of communication built on tapping on the walls. This "tap code" was a simple way to use taps on a wall to spell words.

A five-square-by-five-square grid (see table 14.1) was used with letters corresponding to each box. The letters *c* and *k* share the same box, as they have the same sound. A letter is communicated by tapping two values with a pause between each value. For example,

Table 14.1. Grid used by war prisoners to communicate with one another

	1	2	3	4	5
1	A	B	C/K	D	E
2	F	G	H	I	J
3	L	M	N	O	P
4	Q	R	S	T	U
5	V	W	X	Y	Z

to communicate the letter *m* one would tap on the wall three times, pause, and then tap two times. Tap-tap-tap, pause, tap-tap.

As basic as this was, it was a gift that kept hope alive. The prisoners could share stories, encourage one another, and warn one another about difficult interrogations coming up. Most importantly, they would have their friends by their side in the hell of prison. The code gave the prisoners not only a means to communicate but also a means to still have each other's friendship. In the dark depths of that prison, a reason to keep going was found in community. Telos was found in the other.

As new prisoners came in, they were taught this secret system. One POW said that at the risk of their lives, two fellow prisoners gave him the means to communicate using the tap code. He said these "conversations" were how he was able to retain his pride and sanity through two years of solitary confinement.[2]

Better to risk more torture and possible death than to be alone. Mere taps on the wall from another human kept prisoners sane. Humans are made for other humans. To be alone is to have one's humanity disregarded. Knowing that the taps on the wall, however quiet they may have been, were from another human, had the power to keep the prisoners going. Without them, despair and insanity could set in.

It is not good for man to be alone.

CONNECTED AND ALONE

There is a loneliness epidemic in the modern world, despite supposedly being more connected than ever. We can make calls and send texts, we have zoom and social media, we can travel at speeds that were unthinkable in the past. And yet, we feel alone. Isolated. The digital connections are insufficient. Humans need humans. They need real, embodied interaction. They need to mourn and cry, celebrate and rejoice, pray and sing together. They need face-to-face human relationships.[3]

In 2023 the United States Department of Health and Human Services published a document on the growing problem of loneliness. The document is titled "Our Epidemic of Loneliness and Isolation," with the subhead "The U.S. Surgeon General Advisory on the Healing Effects of Social Connection and Community."[4] Listen to some of the conclusions regarding the relationship between health and loneliness. The document states:

> The lack of social connection poses a significant risk for individual health and longevity. Loneliness and social isolation increase the risk for premature death by 26% and 29% respectively. More broadly, lacking social connection can increase the risk for premature death as much as smoking up to 15 cigarettes a day. In addition, poor or insufficient social connection is associated with increased risk of disease, including a 29% increased risk of heart disease and a 32% increased risk of stroke. Furthermore, it is associated with increased risk for anxiety, depression, and dementia. Additionally, the lack of social connection may increase susceptibility to viruses and respiratory illness.

Loneliness can kill.

Here is more bad news. A quarter of young adults report feeling lonely.[5] Nearly one-third of all adults report feeling lonely once a week.[6] One in ten adults reports feeling lonely all the time.[7] Different studies have different results, with some registering much greater percentages of Americans feeling lonely, but here is the obvious point: we have a connection-and-belonging problem.

For the first time since Gallup has been conducting this poll, less than half of all Americans say they belong to a religious body or community.[8] According to Pew Research, only 16 percent of people say that they feel very attached to their community.[9] The modern person does not belong; they are not a part of something larger than themselves. People are lonely. It's so bad that people are suffering health effects due to isolation. People are literally dying because they do not have "one another."

The church has the answer. Better put, the church *is* the answer. Yet we have Christian slogans emphasizing an individualistic Christianity. Slogans that remove the religious structure and community that give stability and security and tell people all they need is a "personal relationship with Jesus." It is the Christian faith, with its rites, rituals, and practices, that gives the structure that supports the growth of a healthy relationship not only with God but also with "one another." And you need the other. You cannot do it alone.

THE FAITH OF AN OLD MAN

I remember a time when a man in our church had just lost his wife. They had been together for sixty-plus years. They would still hold hands during service, even in their eighties; it was that kind of love. The week she passed away the frail elderly man entered the church. He sat where he usually sat. This time, alone. On the week of his bride's passing, he was in church. Overwhelmed and full of grief . . . he still came to church.

Every Sunday at every church, there are those who don't feel like participating in worship. We all have struggles, doubts, and fears, and it can be all too easy to use them as reasons not to engage in worship. But what that man did that Sunday morning served as a beautiful and powerful example for us all. Whatever reasons we may have had that Sunday to think that it wasn't a good day to worship God, he removed those thoughts. When the music started, the elderly man stood up and raised the hand that used to grasp his wife's hand in worship. In the midst of soul-crushing loss, he worshiped. And when the congregation saw his hands raised, it was as if he was helping them lift theirs as well. His worship was contagious. How could we not sing when this man so full of sorrow stood with lifted hands?

Sometimes in life your faith falters, and you don't feel like getting out of bed to worship God. But by going to church you allow the faith of others to lift your own faith.

There is a story in the Gospel of Mark, a first-century biography of the life of Jesus, that records a miracle. Mark tells us that Jesus was at a home in Capernaum:

> And many were gathered together, so that there was no more room, not even at the door. And he was preaching the word to them. And they came, bringing to him a paralytic carried by four men. And when they could not get near him because of the crowd, they removed the roof above him, and when they had made an opening, they let down the bed on which the paralytic lay. And when *Jesus saw their faith*, he said to the paralytic, "Son, your sins are forgiven." (Mark 2:2-5, italics added)

Did you catch that? Jesus sees *their* faith. Jesus sees the faith of the four men, and he says to the paralytic, "Your sins are forgiven." Now, I am not saying that the paralytic didn't have any faith, and that his faith was not involved in Jesus' pronouncement; nevertheless, what does the text highlight? That the faith of the four friends, at least in some sense and to some degree, played a role.

Jesus would later go on to heal this man of his paralysis as well, which raises another question: How would the paralytic man have even gotten to Jesus if it hadn't been for his friends? There is no healing without the faith of those four men. It does not happen. Their faith was so strong that they climbed onto a roof, broke through this first-century Galilean home, and lowered their friend. Can you imagine the audacity?

Maybe the paralyzed man was one who had little faith. Maybe his own family had given up faith and hope that one day he would walk. Maybe the religious leaders in his community told him that his paralysis was punishment from God. None of that mattered. When the four men broke through the roof by faith, Jesus took notice.

Sometimes you need friends to have faith when you don't.

HUSBAND AND WIFE

The Bible ends the way it begins, with a wedding. In the first pages we see Adam and Eve. In the last pages we see Christ and his church.

> Then I heard what seemed to be the voice of a great multitude, like the roar of many waters and like the sound of mighty peals of thunder, crying out,
>
> > "Hallelujah!
> > For the Lord our God
> >   the Almighty reigns.
> > Let us rejoice and exult
> >   and give him the glory,
> > for the marriage of the Lamb has come,
> >   and his Bride has made herself ready;
> > it was granted her to clothe herself
> >   with fine linen, bright and pure"—

for the fine linen is the righteous deeds of the saints.
(Revelation 19:6-8)

Christ is going to return. Who is he coming back for? His bride. Yes, if you trust in him, that includes you—but the language is important. He is only coming back for *you* because he is coming back for his *bride*: the church. There is only one bride.

God's people constitute the one body, the one bride, the one church. And when God's people gather, he is there with them in a profound way. Of course, God is omnipresent, so he is always with believers in one sense, but he is uniquely with his people when they gather around Word and sacrament, in corporate worship. If each believer is a temple of the Holy Spirit, imagine what it's like when *all* believers gather.

When materialism seems to be turned up louder than usual in your life, the faith of others can raise the volume on what is true. When life feels empty, the faith of others can help fill you. Part of what it means to be human is to exist alongside the other. So, know as an individual that you are the church, but you are the church because you are a part of the church.

And every week we need to gather with the church, because we need each other.

It is not good for us to be alone.

15

The Lord's Prayer

WHAT IF I TOLD YOU there was something nearly every Christian memorized in the early church. These words were not only committed to memory—Christians were also taught to recite them three times a day.[1] Not a single day would pass without these words on the lips of Christians. The words were sacred, and they were to ever be on the heart and mind of the Christian. These are the words:

> Our Father in heaven,
> hallowed be your name.
> Your kingdom come,
> your will be done,
>   on earth as it is in heaven.
> Give us this day our daily bread,
> and forgive us our debts,
>   as we also have forgiven our debtors.
> And lead us not into temptation,
>   but deliver us from evil. (Matthew 6:9-13)

When Jesus is asked how we are to pray, these are the words that he gives. They are words that connect those of us here below on earth with our Father above in heaven. Jesus gives finite humans language to approach the infinite.

Sometimes this prayer is referred to as the "Our Father." This is an appropriate title because not only does the prayer begin with those words, but also those two words have the power in them to fundamentally change you at every level.

Think about it. How is it that little, tiny, insignificant you can call God "Father"? That should shake us at our core. We approach an omnipotent (all powerful), omniscient (all knowing), omnipresent (all present), infinite being . . . as children coming to their father?

What sane person would think they could talk to God like this? The early church father Cyprian of Carthage writes on the utter audacity of calling God "Father." He writes, "How great is the Lord's indulgence! How great His condescension and plenteousness of goodness towards us, seeing that He has wished us to pray in the sight of God in such a way as to call God Father, . . . a name which none of us would dare to venture on in prayer, unless He Himself had allowed us thus to pray!"[2] Where did we get the idea that we can talk to God like this? The answer to that question comes from Jesus. We are not insignificant, we matter.

The joy of Christian living is living as a *child of God*. He is your Father. If you know that you belong to him, it will change everything about you: how you see the world, how you see yourself, and how you see him. Your story fundamentally changes.

You are his! You are his kid no matter what.[3] No matter what has happened to you. No matter what is in your past. No matter what you've done or what's been done to you, you belong to him. He is your father.

There is another truth that naturally flows out of this. Jesus not only teaches us to call on God as Father, but he also begins the prayer by saying "our" Father. Not only do *you* belong to a good Father, but the prayer implies that there are *others*. Every Christian who calls upon God as Father is your brother or sister. You have a Father, and you have a family. A family that is made from people of every tribe, tongue, and nation.

The entire family of God calls on him as Father. Rich and poor, man and woman, Jew and Gentile—no matter the differences, we are bound together in that we all call him Father. Whether a king in a castle or a beggar on the street, the playing field is equal as we approach our God. The king has no more right than the beggar to approach God; in fact, the king and the beggar are brothers.

Calling on God as Father reminds us of who we are and what we are a part of. In a world with so much isolation and division, it can easily feel like we don't really belong or like we are always on the outside. When you call on God as Father you are saying, "I belong." Calling God "Father" declares the true story of who you are, where you are going, and who you belong to.

WORDS OF POWER

There is a tendency for some Christians to have a knee-jerk reaction to memorized prayers. Our culture values being true to "the real you" and being authentic to such a degree that often anything resembling ritualistic prayer is easily looked down on. Some think prayers like the Lord's Prayer are just formulas that do not communicate what is really in the heart. Obviously, memorized prayers can become lifeless words that are done out of obligation, but just because something can be misused does not mean one should throw it out.

Remember who gave us this prayer: Jesus. The transcendent One who is "God with us" gave us these words. Who else knows the "true you" better? Who else could better explicate the human condition? Who better than God himself to tell us how he ought to be approached? The Lord's Prayer is words given to us by God to approach God.

Furthermore, there are times in life when you won't have it in you to pray some "true and authentic" words from the heart. You will be at a loss for words. There are days too sad, too overwhelming, too heavy to muster up the words needed. In those moments, you have been given a prayer that you can say. *Our Father who lives in heaven . . .*

Picture a family in a hospital as they surround their father lying in a bed. The news is bad. He has very little time left. He has lived a life serving Jesus and now before him are his adult children, his grandchildren, and even some great-grandchildren. He is coming in and out of sleep and has very little energy left. As the family finishes saying their goodbyes, there is still one last prayer for the old man to give. He has not the energy for a long prayer, or words that can describe what he is feeling now in these final moments.

So, what does the old man pray?

"Our Father in heaven, hallowed be your name." The prayer is automatic. He does not even have to think about it. He has said these words countless times and will now say them one last time. *"Your kingdom come, your will be done, on earth as it is in heaven."* He is now moments away from seeing his king and the kingdom he has longed for all these years. *"Give us this day our daily bread."* He is grateful that God's hand of blessing enabled him to provide for his family throughout his life. *"And forgive us our debts, as we also have forgiven our debtors."* The old man has no grudges, no unforgiveness in his heart, no bitterness, no one left to forgive because he has lived a life of forgiveness. He knows that he, too, has been forgiven much. *"And lead us not into temptation, but deliver us from evil."* And now the final deliverance. Evil will not touch the old man. Death will not claim him. The old man is a King's kid. He belongs to God.

ROYAL LANGUAGE

The Lord's Prayer is filled with royal language. The Father we address in the prayer is said to have a kingdom, and if one has a kingdom, then they are a king. At first, we might believe that we can easily see and relate to God as King, but trust me: there are problems with this. Americans are anti-king by nature. Our nation began with a revolution against the Crown. It's in our DNA. We vote and we elect, and if we don't like something, we can speak out against it. Even though in this country we love and cherish these rights, it is important to remember that the Christian faith is not a democracy. It is a monarchy. There is a King.

In the 2012 movie adaptation of Victor Hugo's 1862 masterpiece *Les Misérables*, the opening scene begins with this text appearing on the screen: "1815, Twenty-six years after the start of the French Revolution a king is once again on the throne of France."[4]

I remember watching the movie for the first time and automatically being on the side of those who would rebel against the king. At the time, I did not know the historical information surrounding the events, I did not know what good or bad the king had done, and I did not know the motivations of those in rebellion. But it didn't matter; my default position was that the king must be bad.

My reaction was not solely due to my American sentiment. The Bible is filled with bad kings. Even the good kings are, well, sort of bad. The quintessential example of this is, of course, King David. David is the king that all other kings are measured against, and even *he* was an adulterer and a murderer.

But the king in the Lord's Prayer is different. He is a good king. He is the true and good and beautiful king. He loves the citizens of his kingdom. He fights for them and is not against them. This is really good news, but make no mistake about it—he is still a monarch.

This means we don't elect him, we don't make deals with him, we don't bargain with him. The Lord's Prayer reminds us that there is a throne with all authority, there is someone sitting on it, and it is not us.

Of course, all of this is more good news. It will sound bad only to a people who think they are more fit than God to govern the universe. A good king on the throne is what we want. It becomes a joy to give him our allegiance. And once we give him our allegiance, even more good news emerges. Allegiance brings adoption into the king's family, which means all those who call on him as Father are of royal position.

Similar to the word *king*, sometimes our own personal experience with our own earthly fathers can taint the word. Just as someone who has had only bad kings rule over them might be apprehensive toward a new king, so also someone who has had a bad earthly father might shy away from the idea of calling God "Father."

The answer to this dilemma is not to run away from words like *king* and *father*, but rather to let the good King and Father reshape our understanding of what those words ought to feel like. Jesus taught us to pray like this for good reason.

Christian theology has always emphasized the fact that Jesus is both *eternal* and *begotten*. He is begotten of the Father, but eternal and without beginning. There was never a time when Jesus did not exist. What this means is that the Father, who begets the Son, has always been Father. He is the eternal Father. There was never a moment when he was not Father. I know that may be a bit complicated, but the simple point is this: when we say, "Our Father," we are addressing God in a manner that he has always been. He has always been and will always be a good Father.

MEANINGFUL SUFFERING

The Lord's Prayer asks for protection from temptation and evil. Like so many of the practices of the faith we have talked about, it presupposes hardship, struggle, and pain in this life. Life hits hard, and when you think it can't hit any harder, it does. In a materialist story there is no explanation that can give remedy to any of this. What separates your suffering from the suffering of a dying fruit fly except that humans are more complex creatures?

The Lord's Prayer places your suffering in the context of the great story. Humans have rebelled against the good king. However, the good king did not abandon them. He is returning to make things right. His kingdom will come to bear on the kingdoms of the earth. Your endurance and present faithfulness to the world's true king matters. There will be a reckoning. So, in the midst of a world filled with pain and suffering: endure, hold fast, stay the course, and remember who you are, what you belong to, and where you are going.

In the children's fantasy series The Wingfeather Saga by Andrew Peterson, many of these ideas are brought to life in the story of the characters. The Wingfeather Saga tells the story of a royal family. The father, Esben, ruled over the Kingdom of Anniera. As in many of the great stories we tell, the king is betrayed, and the kingdom falls to evil. Esben's wife and children flee the burning castle and are forced to live secret lives as the enemy hunts them down.

The children in this story experience so much pain and suffering but always seem to muster up the strength to push forward. The new world created after the fall of Anniera is one of tyranny. The new overlords crush any seeds of hope. In times like this it's easy to believe nothing good is coming, that the darkness has won, and that the kingdom you long for will never come to be. One night when the light seems incredibly dim, the eldest boy, Janner, is given a letter from his mother written by his father, King Esben, many years prior. It reads:

> Dearest Janner, you've royal blood in your veins, no matter what your name or place in this world. The Maker made you. . . . There are rumors of war. Should Anniera fall, should I fall, remember your homeland. Ancient secrets lie beneath these stones and cities. We mustn't let them fall to evil. One day when you're alone, unsure, doubting yourself, you'll need these words. Remember this: You are Annieran. Your father is a king. You are his son. This is your land, and nothing can change that. Nothing. Know when you read this that your father loves you like no other. Your papa.[5]

This is the love of a father.

The saga has also been made into an animated series, and both times as I read the books and watched the cartoon, I wept. I wept as a father because I thought of my children and the world they face. This world is filled with evil, and they, too, will have to learn to face it. I also wept because in it is the deep longing of my heart and every human heart . . . to know who we are, to know that we are loved, to know that there is a Father who will never stop loving us. This is what the Lord's Prayer teaches us.

There is an ache and longing in the Lord's Prayer, "your kingdom come." We have a desire for this other kingdom. It's like we have an appetite for something we have never eaten before, and a thirst for something we can't quite articulate. Nevertheless, it's there. We long for this place. Truth, goodness, and beauty call out to us from there.

In *The Voyage of the Dawn Treader* by C. S. Lewis, the brave mouse Reepicheep volunteers to sail to the eastern edge of the world in hopes of breaking a curse placed on the seven lords of Narnia. He boldly risks his life in the belief that going past the eastern edge of the world will lead to Aslan's country.

Aslan, creator of Narnia, is the one who Reepicheep has served with his life, and the one whose kingdom little Reepicheep has always yearned to see. There is a deep longing in the mouse. Although sailing to the eastern edge means either Aslan's country or certain death, the mouse is resolute.

He says, "My own plans are made. While I can, I sail east in the *Dawn Treader*. When she fails me, I paddle east in my coracle. When she sinks, I shall swim east with my four paws. And when I can swim no longer, if I have not reached Aslan's country, or shot over the edge of the world into some vast cataract, I shall sink with my nose to the sunrise."[6]

The mouse always had a longing and belief that there was something more . . . don't we all?

INEXHAUSTIBLE TRUTH

The Lord's Prayer is fuel for the Christian. In a very real sense, the Lord's Prayer captures much of what we have been talking about in this book. It's a prayer that brings together so many of the rites, rituals, and practices we have discussed. The prayer reminds us of our true story and who we belong to. It tells us why we matter and what it means to live as a child of God. It reminds us of the time we are in—the present evil age—seeing and waiting for the inbreaking of God's kingdom. It teaches us thanksgiving for daily bread and provision. It reminds us that evil is real, so we must take a side. Allegiance must be given, and faithfulness sustained. It reminds us that we are not alone but part of the family of God. The Lord's Prayer compresses so many of these inexhaustible truths into something that can be memorized and recited so that you never forget the power they hold.

Isn't it strange that a prayer that was given to us by Jesus himself, and memorized and repeated multiple times a day by the first Christians, rarely makes it to the lips of modern Christians? Many Christians have never committed it to memory. Many Christians rarely recite it. This is to our detriment. Our Lord gave us this gift to empower us.

Life can be so painful. People will hurt you. Loved ones will betray you. It will feel as if there is no hope for the world and no good to hope for. You will fail. Your feet will falter. You will want to give up on yourself. Sometimes the darkness is just too heavy.

So, the next time you feel alone, unsure and doubting yourself, remember these words: your Father is a king. You are his child. Nothing can change that. Nothing. You are of royal blood. Not because it runs through your veins, but because you were purchased with it. You are blood bought. You are his kid no matter what.

This changes everything.

Part 3

Practices and Patterns

16

Spirits

THE SEVEN CHAPTERS we covered in part two are not exhaustive. We could talk about other practices, like confession of sin, fasting, prayers in general, almsgiving, and more, but with the help of a local church you can put others into practice as well. The previous seven chapters are meant to serve as a foundation that we would be wise to build on.

But as we enter the final section of this book, I'd like to look at one more piece of the puzzle. If materialism is the dominant story in our culture, then we must ask the question, Who is telling the story? So, I'd like to talk with you about spirits. Specifically, the *spirit of the age*. Because the age we live in *does* have a spirit, and whether we like it or not, we live under it. If we want to apply the practices in this book to our lives, we will need to understand that we are doing so in and under the present spirit of the age. Let's start with a dictionary definition and go from there.

The Collins Dictionary defines *spirit of the age* like this: "The set of ideas, beliefs, practices, behaviors, and aims that is typical of people in a particular period in history."[1] The definition is straightforward, but if we are going to understand the phrase, we will need to reflect deeply on the word *spirit*.

It may not be evident at first, but we use the word *spirit* in a variety of different ways that seemingly have very little in common.

However, on further examination, we can see that there is something binding all these uses together. So, what do we mean when we say *spirit*? Let's look at several examples of how this word is used.

If you grew up in the Christian tradition, you are familiar with the phrase *unclean spirit*. An unclean spirit, or demon, is an immaterial being that seeks malevolent influence in the life of humans. In the Gospel accounts, we see demons exercising influence to such a degree that we are forced to adopt a different type of language to describe this influence. The influence becomes so strong that it changes from influence-like language to possession-like language. There are many passages in Scripture where Jesus confronts someone who is so *under the influence* of one of these spirits that we say, at least in some sense, the spirit is more in control than the person.

Another way we use the word *spirit* is to refer to the immaterial part of a person. For example, when an elderly woman dies, we might hear a grandchild say something like, "We know that her body is still here, but Grandma is now in a better place." What is being said is that part of the person is still here (the body), but another part of them (the spirit) is somewhere else. Humans of all different types of backgrounds speak in this manner.

A third way we use the word *spirit* is to refer to an essential quality or characteristic that influences the entirety of an individual's behavior. For example, you might know a very kind person and thus refer to them as having a "gentle spirit." When we say someone has a gentle spirit, we are saying the essence of their personality is gentle. In other words, whatever the person is doing, they are usually doing it in a gentle manner. It's the invisible quality that manifests itself in all areas of their life. So, we might say that they speak gently, they walk gently, they even argue gently. Likewise, someone might have an "angry spirit." And by that we mean they speak angrily, they argue angrily, they even get angry when they reflect on their anger problem.

A fourth way we use the word is in reference to hard alcohol. While there is a long, mysterious history as to when and why people first started referring to distilled alcohol with this type of language, the fact is, the language chosen is hauntingly accurate. Hard alcohol is like a "spirit" both in the way it is made and in the way it is consumed.

Most alcoholic beverages have low alcohol content. This means that a low percentage of the drink is actually the stuff that will intoxicate you. For example, beer is often around 5 percent alcohol; wine, around 12 percent. Hard alcohol, which is often called a "spirit," is found at a much higher concentration level. Drinks like vodka, tequila, whiskey, and others usually come in around the 40 percent alcohol content level and carry the "spirit" name. How are these types of drinks able to acquire such potency? Because they go through an intense distillation process.

Distillation occurs when a drink with lower alcohol content is boiled in order to separate the alcohol from the nonalcoholic substance. Alcohol has a lower boiling point, so it will begin to steam and turn into a gas before water and the rest of the liquid do. As the drink boils, the alcohol steams and rises like a spirit, leaving the "body" of the drink behind. Picture an old cartoon with a character like Wile E. Coyote falling off a cliff and dying. In a comical manner, a little, blue spirit appears above his body, and he begins to float up. In the case of alcohol, distillers catch the spirit (steam), isolate it, and cool it back down to return it to liquid form. This new liquid is the "spirit." Distillation, then, is a way of extracting the essence of the drink so that you have its isolated and more potent form.

Additionally, we call it a spirit because the substance of the spirit can influence your behavior. When someone drinks too much, the spirit alters their actions. When consumed in moderation, the effects wear off quickly, and you can return to your usual self within hours. However, if you act recklessly and drink before you drive, you are allowing the spirit to alter your behavior and ability to drive. When someone is caught doing this, we say the person is *driving under the influence*.

The consequences of drinking and driving are terrifying, but here is the good news: if you don't want to have the spirit's influence in your life, you simply don't drink it. The key here is that the spirit can only influence you if you invite it in.

But what happens when a spirit is invited in again and again, year after year? In that case the spirit takes up a sort of permanent residency in the person. It molds them and shapes them to such a degree that you might hear a loved one say, "That's not the person I knew."

At first, you abuse the spirit. Then, in a sinister exchange, the spirit begins to abuse you.

Like an unclean spirit tormenting its prisoner, the spirit so warps an individual over time that their new character is unrecognizable when compared to the old. We let something in, and slowly but surely, over time, it changes us. We are no longer under its *influence*, we are under its *control*.[2]

The spirit needs a host body to have any influence. In the song "Necktie Remedy" by Project 86, singer Andrew Schwab captures the idea well. In its opening lyrics, alcohol is personified and given a voice. The alcohol says, "Make me into something, give me a body. . . . Let me out the bottle, make me into someone."[3]

In this song, alcohol is an immaterial being looking for a host body to exercise influence over. Does this sound familiar? Recall our first usage of the word *spirit*: the unclean spirit. Remember how we said that a person can be so under the influence of a spirit that we no longer use words like *influence* but rather words like *control*? It appears that some of our uses of the word *spirit* have more in common than initially thought. But there's more.

This final use of the word *spirit* is going to take some time to explain. It is a bit strange, but stick with me—it's worth it. Let's talk about *team spirit*. What is team spirit? Think of this spirit like an immaterial force that influences a group's behavior based on an agreed upon aim. This agreed upon aim—namely, winning the game—creates a unity and a shared energy that can strengthen or weaken depending on how the team is doing. Furthermore, this energy can create patterns of behavior that we might describe as having something like a gravitational pull. The greater the energy is, the greater pull it has. And once you are in its orbit, you, too, begin to replicate the pattern, thus increasing the influence and power of the spirit. This might make more sense with an example.

Imagine you are at a basketball game. Let's say it is game seven in the NBA Finals. And let's also say that your team, the home team, is down fifteen points at the start of the fourth quarter. If you aren't familiar with basketball, being down fifteen points at the start of the fourth quarter is bad, but it is not insurmountable. As the fourth quarter begins, what do you suppose the energy is like in the stadium? Is it one filled with excitement and anticipation of the championship that is about to be won? No. The mood is down. The energy is low. You are upset. You tell yourself, *I paid a ton of money to be here only to watch these clowns blow it!* (Everyone is, of course, an expert on how the team should have played in these moments.) Your mind begins to drift off . . . *If they don't hit the start of the fourth quarter strong, then I'll leave early to beat the nightmare of grouchy people all leaving the parking lot at the same time.*

The fourth quarter begins and the team's best player and fan favorite shoots a three-pointer, but the ball rims out. You tell yourself, *C'mon man, just get an easy two and try to close the gap.* At the other end of the court, your team plays some decent defense and gets a stop, and now the ball is in the hands of the fan-favorite superstar again. Again, he throws up a three-pointer. The crowd is silent, holding their breath, hoping for a miracle. Even the atheists are throwing up some prayers at this point . . . but . . . air ball. The home crowd lets out a collective breath of extreme disappointment. Someone sitting next to you, who also appears to be an expert, yells, "Trade the bum! He's got no game." At this point, you convince yourself that this might be a good time to start heading to the parking lot.

But then the superstar makes a terrific steal on defense and sprints down the court. Without hesitation he shoots another three! And this time, something different happens: it goes in. Now, suddenly, there is a glimmer of hope. The stadium is still a bit quiet, but people are watching the game more intensely. Next, another defensive stop! The superstar dribbles down the court and, with a hand in his face, shoots another three. Nothing but net! The entire stadium jumps to their feet. "We are within nine points!" you scream out loud.

Now, let's pause for a moment. What just happened? A man on a basketball court made a ball go in a hoop. Keep in mind, this man is very far away from you because you can't afford good seats and you're way in the back. Nevertheless, something done on a court by one individual has changed the entire atmosphere in the arena. There is a new type of energy in the stadium now. What is being done on that court by this one person somehow influences every single individual in the arena. This influence is somehow exercising its power over thousands of people. Hearts are racing, people are up on their feet, and they're chanting at the top of their lungs: "Defense! Defense! Defense!"

Out of nowhere, you are caught up in the spirit of the team. The team spirit is creating energy, and not just for the people watching. The more the crowd cheers, the better the team seems to play. The energy goes both ways. The more one side displays the energy, the greater the energy on the other side. What a strange phenomenon.

Let's go even further with this. Let's say the only reason why you are at this game is because your wife bought both of you tickets for your anniversary. She's not a basketball fan, but she knows how much you love the game, so she surprised you. Now, when I say she is not a fan, I mean that she knows so little about the game that you had to remind her which team to root for at the start of the game.

But something happened in the fourth quarter. At some point when people were standing on their feet chanting "Defense," she actually joined in. Before this, she was a passive observer of the game taking place on the court, but somehow the spirit in the arena drew her in. She is no longer a passive observer; she is now an active participant in the spirit of the team. The team spirit in the room had a gravitational pull. The more that people were drawn into the spirit's orbit, the stronger the spirit became. At a certain point, even those individuals at the game who did not care one bit about the sport of basketball began screaming "Defense!" at the top of their lungs.

Have you ever seen this? Have you ever experienced this? As more and more people are pulled into a pattern of behavior, the pull gets stronger. At first, 50 percent of the stadium is on their feet, but then 70, then 90. And by the final minutes it's nearly impossible not to be on your feet and cheering. The pattern of behavior gets adopted and repeated, and every time this happens, its power grows.

Now, a question: Can certain events taking place on a basketball court trigger a change of energy that spreads throughout an entire arena? Can this energy become so strong that unless you actively resist it, you, too, will get caught up in it? The answer is yes, of course. If this can happen during a basketball game, can it happen in a culture? Can a spirit of the times do something similar to the spirit of the team? Can patterns of behavior be replicated again and again by more and more individuals so that at a certain point it becomes very difficult to resist them?[4] Can people as a whole begin to believe certain things and hold to certain values not because they logically thought through them but because they are simply caught up in the spirit of the age? Can *you* live under the story that a spirit is telling to such a degree that, without even thinking, you adopt the tenets of that story?

To resist the pattern is nearly impossible.

Is this sounding something like the world we all live in? Is this sounding like working at In-N-Out Burger, where there is almost nothing you can do to fight the fact that if you work at In-N-Out, you will at least to some degree *smell* like In-N-Out?

Let's gather some of our findings together and see what ideas rise to the surface. There are forces, substances, and intelligences (often immaterial) that can change you. They are external forces that exert influence over you and have the ability to change your behavior. These spirits create patterns, and as the patterns are repeated, their pull becomes stronger.

All of this may still sound a bit weird, but let me give you a concrete example from our place and time that demonstrates how this works.

A SPIRIT OF LUST

We might say that in our culture there is a "spirit" of lust. Sex is everywhere, and it has become an all-consuming power in the world we live in. One of the primary feeders of this beast is pornography. With that in mind, let's do a quick thought experiment. Picture a man who is married with kids. Unfortunately, like so many fathers in our culture, he begins to look at pornography on his computer. Slowly, over time, he consumes more and more of it until at some point it crosses the line into addiction. With the father constantly participating in this behavior, do you think his thirteen-year-old son is now more or less likely to be exposed to pornography? The answer is obvious, right? Going further, if the son is exposed and begins to look at pornography, is the son more likely to get addicted like his father? Again, the answer is obvious.

Let's take this one step further. With this young adolescent now addicted to pornography, when the thirteen-year-old has friends over at the house to hang out, is he more or less likely to expose some of his friends to pornography?

See the pattern?

A behavior that's picked up by the father and then repeated by the son is now a replicating pattern that is likely to be passed on. Once the pattern is picked up by the son's friends, just imagine how many more times that pattern will be replicated. How many other friends or brothers or sisters will get caught in the gravitational pull?

Now imagine living in a culture where there are countless patterns, all being replicated, broadcast, and amplified at every level of society. How could anyone resist the gravitational pull of the pattern? Still worse, even if you hate the pattern, the mere fact that you live within a time and place where that pattern is broadcast will cause you either to actively resist it or be consumed by it. There is no neutrality. There is no safe zone. *Resist or replicate* like the others.

These types of replicating patterns can manifest themselves at every level, from ideological issues to habits around the family table. Picture a family of five sitting around a dinner table. Everyone is talking and having a great time discussing their day when suddenly the fifteen-year-old takes out her phone and begins to look at social media. Pause for a moment. What is the likelihood that within the next thirty seconds another family member is going to be tempted to take out their phone as well? The mere introduction of an image of a phone at the table can send signals to everyone else at the table that they, too, should check their notifications. Again, a behavior creates patterns that are replicated.

Now let's take all of this with us and return to our original phrase "spirit of the age." The "spirit of the age" is the set of ideas, beliefs, practices, behaviors, and aims that is typical of people in a particular period in history.

Does our culture have a set of ideas, beliefs, practices, behaviors, and aims? Have you seen how the more a population adopts new behaviors and values that the feeling to just go along with the flow increases? Have you ever seen someone say they believe something that they have not truly thought through, something they sort of just absorbed from the culture at large? Have you ever seen someone believe or behave in a manner that just five years prior they would have said was immoral and wrong?

The gravitational pull is real. It sucks you in, and it *will* change you. The spirit of the age comes for us all.

So, what are we to do when we know that we live in a culture filled with harmful spirits that create patterns to capture and destroy us? How can we live in and under the spirit of the age? We must resist the pattern.

The apostle Paul, writing to Christians living in Rome two thousand years ago who were dealing with a different spirit of the age, said this:

"I appeal to you therefore, brothers, by the mercies of God, to present your bodies as a living sacrifice, holy and acceptable to God, which is your spiritual worship. Do not be conformed to this world, but be transformed by the renewal of your mind, that by testing you may discern what is the will of God, what is good and acceptable and perfect" (Romans 12:1-2).

Focus in on the beginning of the second verse, "Do not be conformed to this world." Let's explore another important word from the ancient world. The word translated "world" comes from the Greek word *aiōn*. *Aiōn* can be defined as "world, era, age, time, period, or universe," or, perhaps more meaningful to us, something like "the world systems and structures that govern the world." This is why some versions of the Bible translate *aiōn* in Romans 12 as "patterns of this world."

Paul is saying to Christians who are trying to live faithfully at the center of the empire, and thus at the center of the spirit of the age, "Do not be conformed to the patterns of this world."

But that's easier said than done, right?

Thankfully, Paul does not leave us with only a "do not." He tells us what we ought to do. Examine the verse again. We are to present *our bodies as living sacrifices*. We are to be *transformed by the renewal of our minds*. We are to discern the will of God, *knowing what is good, acceptable, and right*.

What might that look like in dealing with some of the spirits of *our* age that we previously discussed? Let's go back to our example of the father looking at pornography. What if the father knew he lived in a culture with a spirit of lust? What if he told himself this spirit is not only coming for him but will come for his children? Furthermore, what if he understood that if the spirit captures him, it would be more likely to capture his kids as well?

With this awareness the father sets out to wage war on the spirit of lust. He makes sure all passwords on devices are shared between him and his wife. Phones and tablets are to be used only in family spaces; they are not allowed to be taken into secrecy. He gets software installed on all devices, which helps him and his family in their fight against the spirit. He regularly talks about whatever struggles he has in this area with friends that he trusts. He even refuses to watch some movies, that, although not necessarily pornographic, might still feed the spirit and give it power.

Sounds radical, right?

It's not. Not when you've seen the lives that I've seen ruined by pornography.

Now let's go back to a question we've already asked. If the dad does all this to protect himself and resist the spirit of lust, do you think it is now more or less likely that his thirteen-year-old is not exposed to pornography? The answer is obvious. The son is now less likely to be exposed and thus less likely to pick up an addiction. To be clear, it does not guarantee it. It does not save the son completely from the spirit of the age, but it does give him a better chance. The father did his part to ensure the protection of his son. And with the son not picking up this habit, it is clearly also less likely that he will show his friends that type of content.

What happened in all of this? The father broke the pattern. By doing this, the gravitational pull of the spirit was weakened in his house. Now imagine if he was not the only father to break the pattern, but tens of thousands of fathers began breaking the pattern. What might happen to the power of that spirit? What might happen to the strength of that spirit?

It would weaken.

And as the power of the spirit becomes weaker, more individuals have a fighting chance of not getting caught in its orbit. This is why it is of utmost importance that we resist the spirits and break the pattern. Not just for our own sake, but for others around us, including those we love.

The materialist spirit is a powerful one, and its story is repeated at nearly every institutional level. Sure, there are many other spirits at work, but the dominant story for some time now is the one materialism tells. We live in the ecosystem it has created, and in innumerable ways it shapes how we think. The materialist story says that each of us is just a body. How might that story shape sexual ethics? It says there is no final judge that humans will have to answer to. How might that shape how we treat our friends, neighbors, or even enemies? It says there is no ultimate telos of humans. How will that not rob our lives of meaning? These types of questions could be asked in countless areas of human life. The influence of the materialist story is all-encompassing.

At this point, you may feel overwhelmed at the power of the various spirits of the age; the tasks before you may seem insurmountable. Well,

I have bad news: it's going to get worse. So far, I have been talking only in materialist terms. Everything I have said could be affirmed by a staunch atheist. Yes, I used the term *spirit*; but the way I defined it, one need not even believe in God or any spiritual realities. You don't need to believe in a God or a spiritual realm to believe in a spirit of the age as I defined above. One could simply observe these patterns and see how their influence can grow or weaken in strength.

I have not, however, gone far enough in disclosing the inner working of these spirits. And to these inner workings, the Bible gives a far more sinister origin story. The Bible says the problem is far worse and far darker than what mere material origins can account for. Materialism never gives us the full story.

The Bible says that the spirits of the age are influenced by . . . guess what? *Spirits.*

> Put on the whole armor of God, that you may be able to stand against the schemes of the devil. For we do not wrestle against flesh and blood, but against the rulers, against the authorities, against the cosmic powers over this present darkness, against the spiritual forces of evil in the heavenly places. Therefore take up the whole armor of God, that you may be able to withstand in the evil day, and having done all, to stand firm. (Ephesians 6:11-13)

Materialism is insufficient to explain evil in the world. And when it comes to understanding the spirit of the age, materialism falls short. Paul says, "Make no mistake about it, there are spirits that influence the spirit of the age."

SPIRITS BEHIND THE SPIRITS

Did you notice how epic and grand the language was in the verses from Ephesians? Paul speaks of cosmic powers, of spiritual forces of evil that wage war in heavenly places. This is clearly no small matter.

At first glance it seems even more of a futile fight. You might be thinking, *The patterns were strong enough already, but now you are telling me there are 'cosmic evil powers' at work? What could I possibly do to stand against that?* The answer is found in the very verse that reveals the evil we are up against. Ephesians tells us to stand firm and put on the armor of God. What are the pieces of the armor of God? Nothing more or less than simple acts of Christian living: truth, righteousness, faith, the Word of God, and more. And how do we empower things like faith, righteousness, and knowledge of the Word of God? Simply stated, by participating in the God-ordained practices of the church.

Enlist and swear allegiance in baptism; receive Communion, and remember you live in the present evil age but are awaiting the age to come; sing; pray; give thanks; read the Bible; and pour yourself into a local church. This is how we wage war in the heavenly places. Our weapons are not of this world; they come from above.

There is hope. In the same way the spirits in the heavenly places can influence us way down here, so can we, by daily acts of faithfulness, influence what occurs up there, thereby truly breaking the patterns of the world.

What does the current spirit of our age look like? It is a depressed, lonely, isolating, meaningless, purposeless spirit. It is a godless age. It is a nihilistic age. It is a confusing and chaotic age. It is an age where men call good, evil—and evil, good. It is a spirit that says, "You are alone in the universe. You have no purpose. You do not matter. There is nothing above and nothing below." It says, "Your feet wander aimlessly on a planet that wanders aimlessly through a cosmos without telos."

Know this, deep in your bones: *that spirit is a liar.*

The church for two thousand years has given us the tools to counter this, to resist the spirits of whatever age we find ourselves in and to empower us for a life of meaning. We must cling to the practices of those who came before us. It sustained them through the worst that life could throw at them. Imagine what would happen if we allowed those practices to form and shape us. What would emerge? What type of person would *you* become if you devoted yourself to the rites, rituals, and practices of the Christian faith on an ongoing, consistent basis? That version of you is waiting to be brought out of the shadows and into the light.

17

The Stone and the Sculptor

PEOPLE OFTEN THINK THEY ARE pretty good morally speaking compared to others.[1] We often think we are generally honest, fair, and virtuous. We think we are the type of people who, for the most part, do the right thing. Enter Paul.

Writing to Christians in the city of Ephesus, Paul tells his readers something that, by our modern standards and sensibilities, sounds incredibly offensive. Read it slowly:

> And you were dead in the trespasses and sins in which you once walked, following the course of this world, following the prince of the power of the air, the spirit that is now at work in the sons of disobedience—among whom we all once lived in the passions of our flesh, carrying out the desires of the body and the mind, and were by nature children of wrath, like the rest of mankind. (Ephesians 2:1-3)

Let's list off what Paul says, just so we are clear. You were dead in sin, you followed the course of the world, you followed the devil, you lived according to the passion of your flesh, and thus by nature were children of wrath. Wow. Each one of those phrases is worth looking at to see just how hard-hitting Paul's claims are.

First, "you were dead in the sins in which you once walked." It's easy to miss but the images are almost contradictory. Paul says that you were dead, but at the same time, strangely, somehow walking.

Hmm, *walking dead men* . . . does this sound familiar? It's the image of a zombie-like life.

For a Jewish thinker like Paul, when he speaks of a "walk" he is speaking about how you live in light of God's law. Today, Christians might use the word in a similar manner and ask, "How is your walk with Jesus?" What they are essentially trying to get at is "How are you doing with your relationship with God?" In Hebrew, the word that faithful Jews might use for this type of talk is *halakh* or *halakhah*. Halakhah is how one walks in light of the sum total of God's law. For Jews in Paul's day, when thinking about God's laws, they would immediately think of the Torah. The Torah is the first five books of the Bible, which contain 613 rules, laws, commandments, and statutes for Israel to live by. It is important to note that Torah and these 613 laws were not seen as cold, dry, and lifeless rules that God held over his people. Rather, the Torah was the book that taught you how to walk in the life God offered his people. It was a path, a mode of being that brought joy. Yes, they were rules, but they were also paths of righteousness.

Asking someone about their *halakhah* would be something similar to "How are you living in light of God's good law, and how is your relationship with him?" But notice what Paul says about the state of humanity apart from God. Your *halakhah* is a "dead-in-sin" type of walk. It's an inverted and evil walk. It's the opposite of the life that God intended for you to have. Pretty depressing, but it gets worse.

Paul then says you follow the "course of this world." With the previous chapter in mind, take a guess at what Greek word Paul employs for "course of this world." That's right, *aiōn*. Paul is talking about the "spirit of the age," both the powers and the patterns at work in our current age. Paul's accusation is simple: you follow the course of this world. You are caught up in its gravitational pull. Even more so, he says that you follow the course of the world because you follow "the prince of the power of the air."

Remember, the spirits and patterns down here are influenced by the spirits above. Paul now speaks of the chief of the malevolent spirits: Satan, the devil, the accuser, the serpent of old. It's easy for modern people saturated in a materialist framework to shy away from this stuff, but keep in mind that the belief in spiritual beings was not only believed but presupposed by the vast majority of people who have ever lived. Historically speaking, materialism is the minority position but the default position of our current culture.

Paul is making the incredibly offensive claim that the world is under the spirit of the age and under the influence of evil spiritual beings. And it gets even worse. Paul says that humanity does all of this because humanity wants it like this. He says we do what we do and live in this manner because at our core, this is the "passion of our own flesh." The passions of our flesh are our own wants, longings, and desires. In other words, we walk in the evil patterns of the world because we like them.

At this point, it's all starting to feel like a boxing match gone terribly wrong. Paul is in the ring and is hitting his opponent again and again. In this case, his opponent is us—humanity as a whole. There is no counterpunch. This fight is one-sided. The jabs, the hooks, the uppercuts just keep coming. He says, "You were dead in sin." Jab. "You followed the course of the world." Uppercut. "You followed the devil." Jab. "And you did all of this because you liked it!" Hook! Someone should probably throw in the towel because there is very little hope at this point . . . but the verse goes on.

Paul ends the barrage with maybe the worst of it. He says, because of all of this, you were "children of wrath." Say that phrase to yourself again: "children of wrath." It's a disturbing phrase, isn't it? It feels this way because *children* and *wrath* seem like two words that should never be next to each other. The word *children* typically elicits thoughts and images of innocence, so it is difficult, even disorienting, for us to see it placed alongside the word *wrath*. Nevertheless, this is exactly what Paul is doing. He is going for the knockout punch here.

"You are the walking dead, following the spirit of the age, serving the devil; you do this because you like it, and by nature are thus children of wrath."

Ouch.

OCEANS AND COFFINS

There is an image that is sometimes used to describe how Christ saves us from the hopeless condition of Ephesians 2:1-3. It speaks of a person's state before God in their life. Imagine you can't swim, and you are drowning in the middle of the ocean. You scream for help, but no one comes. You flail your arms in every possible direction trying to keep yourself afloat, but to no avail. Your head now begins to bob up and down as you submerge again and again. You are in absolute panic mode feeling you have no hope. As your body tires and just as you are about to go completely under for the final time, you cry out one last time. All of a sudden, someone grabs your hand. The man brings you on a boat and gives you a warm blanket. The man is, of course, Jesus.

This story and others like it give a simple way of looking at how God intervenes in people's lives. And although I think these illustrations are helpful, I don't think they go far enough. They don't fully capture the situation Paul is articulating.

So let me give you another image. This image is not one of drowning in water but one of being buried alive. Imagine you are six feet under, in a coffin but still conscious. You are screaming into the darkness hoping that someone—anyone—will hear you. In the darkness, panic sets in as you realize that at a certain point you will run out of air, and in this state of panic you begin to claw frantically at the wood of your coffin, illogically hoping that it might help provide an escape. But there is no escape—only darkness and the confines of the coffin. With the remaining sanity you have, you try to calm yourself. You tell yourself, *I have limited air, and I need to slow my breathing to make it last longer.*

Your legs can move only a couple of inches, and your arms even less. The confines of the coffin make the dread that much greater.

Soon you begin to sense that the air feels a little different. It no longer feels as life-giving to your lungs. You realize it's running out. The panic comes flooding back. You scream, yell, cry, and claw, but to no avail. *Help! Help! Please!!* The panic overtakes you and you weep alone in the darkness. You are breathing differently now, almost as if there were a thick blanket over your mouth. And even though you are breathing as deeply as possible, it doesn't seem to stop the suffocation.

As the darkness overtakes you, you begin to hear something. A thump. Maybe you are losing it, maybe you are going crazy . . . but then again, thump. Suddenly you begin to hear what sounds like digging. You would scream but you lack the energy to do so. And then, the impossible: you hear the sound of a shovel breaking through your coffin. Thump! Thump! Thump! And then you see a small crack, light begins to break through, and you breathe in the fresh air while gasping like a newborn baby taking its first breath.

The shovel keeps pounding away and soon a big enough hole opens for you to lift your head. Your eyes begin to adjust to the light and now another hole opens for your arms to break free. The light is blinding, but your eyes do their best to adjust.

As you gather yourself you begin to look at the one who rescued you. As you look at the face of your salvation, something unexpected occurs. You being to scream. You panic. You begin to grab whatever wood and dirt you can get your hands on and throw it back on top of yourself. You put your head and arms back in the coffin. You are frantic again, but frantic to bury yourself, to hide back in your coffin— anything to escape the one who has freed you. Rather than reach for your savior's extended hand, in terror you go back to the coffin.

What is going on?

You try to bury yourself again because the terror of the one rescuing you is greater than the terror of the coffin.

This is confusing, but it is critical to understand.

There is a good so good that the terror it brings is greater than evil . . . because when you see this goodness you realize you have more in common with evil than with it. You are more akin to darkness, more a child of malice than anything remotely bearing any semblance to the light.

And the radiance of this good is brighter than a thousand suns. To even attempt to look at this light is blinding to the eyes. This is why, when the ancient Hebrew prophets encountered this goodness, they were struck dead in fear. One prophet, on seeing the presence of God, said, "Woe is me! for I am undone" (Isaiah 6:5 KJV). The Hebrew word here for "undone" is *damah*. It means "to cease to be" or "to be utterly destroyed." It is something like "coming apart at the fabric of your being."

Even when Christ digs you out of the coffin, you still run and hide. You do this because you don't see your Savior, you see your enemy. You see that the terror of the one digging you out is greater than the coffin. God pursues, we run. This pattern can be seen throughout Scripture and all of history: Adam, why are you hiding? Cain, where is your brother? Abraham, where is Sarah? David, where is Uriah?

Like children in a garden afraid of the father who gave them his image, we run; we hide.

And so, we were dead in our sins. We followed the spirit of the age and thus followed both the course of this world and the serpent of old. We did this because of the passion of our own flesh. Because of this we were not children of light, but children of wrath. Our eyes could not handle the light. We were terrified of it. Even if we were rescued from the coffin, we would hide ourselves all over again.

It is in the midst of this seemingly insurmountable darkness and hopelessness that Scripture provides the greatest of news. Immediately after Paul gives us the horrible news, he gives us the great news:

"But God, being rich in mercy, because of the great love with which he loved us, even when we were *dead in our trespasses, made us alive* together with Christ—by grace you have been saved" (Ephesians 2:4-5, italics added).

But God.

Even in our most dreadful state, God, who is rich in mercy, because of the *great love with which he loved us*, made us alive. God changes the story.

He broke through the coffin, and when we screamed and panicked and tried to go back in, he waited patiently, allowing our eyes to adjust, speaking words of tenderness to our terrified soul. Like a loving parent comforting their crying child, he said, "It's okay, my sweet son." "It's okay, my sweet daughter." "Father is here, and he loves you. No more running, no more hiding. No more darkness. No more night. You are mine."

And as the words of the Father slowly but surely calm your spirit, you feel his hand take hold of yours, and you trust. You are pulled up from the earth and from your coffin, and you feel the embrace of the One you have been *hiding from* but *longing for* your entire life.

You were dead and without hope.

But God.

GREAT NEWS

Just as the bad news got worse, now the good news gets even better.

In Ephesians 2:8-10, Paul goes on to say, "For by grace you have been saved through faith. And this is not your own doing; it is the gift of God, not a result of works, so that no one may boast. For we are his workmanship, created in Christ Jesus for good works, which God prepared beforehand, that we should walk in them."

Why does God save us? Because he loves us. He is rich in mercy and with great love gives us grace. And as great as this all is, there is more. Paul says it is not only that we are made alive in Christ, but also we become his "workmanship." This now brings us to the final old word we will look at.

Workmanship.

The Greek word here translated "workmanship" is *poiēma*. Because our English word *poem* comes from this word, and because when pronounced the two words sound so similar, many times people take this word to mean "poem." You might have heard someone say something like "Ephesians is telling us that we are the very poetry of God." Although that may sound beautiful, it's just not true; that is not what this word means. *Poiēma* did eventually get used in this manner, but that is not how the word worked in the first-century koine Greek that Paul was using. Do not fret though, there is still beauty to be found in this word.

When Paul used the word, it simply meant to "make something." The word is used when a craftsman creates something. Picture a sculptor. He begins with a marble slab. Just a big block of stone. To the naked eye, it is just a big rock. No special character, no obvious design, nothing that you would ever put on display for the world to marvel at.

But in the hands of the right craftsman, in the hands of the master sculptor, something new is brought into reality. The sculptor sees and knows the *telos* of the stone. He has its end goal in mind. However, he must work to bring out the hidden reality. Everything necessary to bring about a masterpiece is right there in the stone, hidden to the normal eye.

So, what does the sculptor do? He takes the chisel and gets to work. Some of the hits are strong, breaking away big chunks of stone, while other hits only chip away small pieces from the large rock. At times the chisel appears to barely kiss a piece of the stone, seemingly removing nothing to the untrained eye. But the master craftsman sees and takes away the smallest of unneeded material. The sculptor sometimes blows on the stone, removing newly formed dust. At other times the sculptor works for hours with what appears to be very little progress; but again, the master craftsman knows exactly what he is doing.

Slowly but surely an image is emerging. The block of stone is revealing its telos; the sculptor is bringing it out.

Figure 17.1 features a picture of a marble statue finished in the early 1850s by Giovanni Strazza. In one sense, this is just a piece of stone. But as you can see, it is also so much more. Strazza somehow made rock appear translucent. This statue of the Virgin Mary is magical in the sense that somehow you see her face, but you see it through a stone veil. Incredible. Somehow, Strazza gives the viewer the ability to see through a stone veil and behold the beauty of a young Mary behind it.

When you look at this magnificent work of art, just imagine how many chisel hits it might have required. How many times were pieces of rock removed? How many times did Strazza blow away the dust so he could take the smallest of chisels to bear on the rock, bringing about the tiniest of details?

In one sense, it's just a rock. But in the hands of the craftsman, it becomes a masterpiece. This is his workmanship. And what does a craftsman do after the job is done? He puts his work on display for the world to see.

Figure 17.1. Giovanni Strazza's *The Veiled Virgin*

We are his workmanship.

We are dust, made not of rock but earth. We were made from the earth and to the earth we will return. But in another sense, we are so much more than mere dirt. There is a craftsman who brings out his telos in us. He does not see mere dust; he sees his workmanship. An image, his image, meant to go on display.

How do we let him chisel away at us? How do we let him blow away unneeded material?

How are we formed and shaped and made to be all we were meant to be? We submit ourselves to the shaping of the master's hand. We trust him and his ways.

The effects of materialism are soul crushing. We humans were never meant to live in the ecosystem it created. It's suffocating. We need a different type of air to breathe. We long for meaning, we hunger for purpose, we yearn to know that we matter. As a pastor I have seen people break out of the world of materialism. I have seen them go from emptiness to fullness. I have seen them cultivate a life of meaning. I have seen them discover who they are, why they matter, and how to navigate this world.

How? By submitting themselves to the God-ordained practices of the church. Day after day, year after year. Soon, something begins to emerge. Things begin to line up and make sense. The hidden character of the statue begins to reveal itself and so many of the questions are resolved. The practices of the church cultivate meaning. In those practices you find aim and purpose. They give you a hierarchy of values. In finding a great telos above, smaller instances of telos emerge below.

The rites, rituals, and practices of the Christian faith are the means by which God brings out the hidden. They may not be new and trendy, but our ancestors learned to faithfully use them. They are the God-ordained tools of the master craftsman. Sometimes they can feel as if they are not working, and that they have no power in them. Trust the hand of the craftsman; he is removing the smallest particles of dust to work in the tiniest of corners.

Life is filled with meaning and purpose. The truth, goodness, and beauty that you experience and long for has a source. Materialism has blinded us, but the good news is that the Christian faith has the tools to give sight to the blind. Telos is revealed as God shapes us; the character of the statue is brought out of the stone.

You are dust, but you are dust made in his image. You are his workmanship.

WHEN LIFE FEELS EMPTY

What are you to do in the age of materialism? How are you to live in our culture's story, a story without telos, a story that tells you your feet wander aimlessly on a planet without purpose?

Resist the spirit of the age. Look up!

You are not a horizontal human. You were made to stand tall, to reach for the heavens. Understand and practice what our ancestors in the faith did.

Sing. Regularly make your entire being a resonant chamber of worship.

Recall your baptism and remember when you first *pledged allegiance.*

Know what time it is. Communion declares you live between the cross and the return. Remain faithful and endure.

Remember the will of God for you is to give thanks. So, *give thanks every day*, and know that his mercies are new every morning.

Read the Bible. It's not only true; it's *more* than true. Live within the story it tells.

Commit to a body of people. *Go to church.* The people there need you, and you need them.

Keep these words ever on your lips: *"Our Father who lives in heaven."*

Do not be conformed to the patterns of this world but be transformed by the renewing of your mind.

And maybe, most of all, never forget who you belong to. Never forget your true story. You are forever and always a good-news person. No matter what this life throws at you, and no matter how hard it hits . . .

Your life matters. It means something.

You were dead in sin and without hope. But God, who is rich in mercy, rescued you.

You have a Father. He loves you. This is his world. And you belong to him.

Notes

1. A TRAGIC STORY

[1] Michael Heisman, "Suicide Note," September 18, 2010, 1875, accessed June 10, 2024, https://archive.org/details/MitchellHeismanSuicideNote.
[2] Heisman, "Suicide Note," 1861.
[3] Heisman, "Suicide Note," 20.
[4] "Suicide Rates on the Rise," State Health Access Data Assistance, June 2020, www.shadac.org/sites/default/files/publications/2020_STATE-Suicide-brief.pdf.
[5] "Provisional Drug Overdose Counts," Centers for Disease Control, accessed January 2, 2025, www.cdc.gov/nchs/nvss/vsrr/drug-overdose-data.htm.
[6] "Drug Overdose Deaths: Facts and Figures," National Institute on Drug Abuse, accessed January 2, 2025, https://nida.nih.gov/research-topics/trends-statistics/overdose-death-rates#Fig1.
[7] John Wolfson, "Why Are We So Lonely?," *Boston College Magazine*, Winter 2024, www.bc.edu/bc-web/sites/bc-magazine/winter-2024-issue/features/why-are-we-so-lonely-.html.
[8] Martin Monto, Nick McRee, and Frank Deryck, "Nonsuicidal Self-Injury Among a Representative Sample of US Adolescents, 2015," Pub Med, August 2018, https://pubmed.ncbi.nlm.nih.gov/29927642.

2. TELOS

[1] At some point I heard a similar analogy but with a Waffle House rather than In-N-Out Burger, but I can't seem to find the person who originally said it.
[2] Reddit, "r/innout," accessed May 15, 2024, www.reddit.com/r/innout/comments/1b8ow0y/is_it_just_me_or_can_you_guys_still_smell_in_n/.
[3] Pliny the Elder, *The Natural History of Pliny* (vol. 1-6), complete ed., (e-artnow), Kindle, chap. 21.
[4] C. S. Lewis, *Surprised by Joy: The Shape of My Early Life* (New York: Harper-Collins, 1956), 254, Kindle.

[5] Viktor E. Frankl, *Man's Search for Meaning* (Boston: Beacon Press, 2006), 76, Kindle, translated by Frankl from Fredrich Nietzsche, *The Twilight of the Idols*, Maxim 12.

[6] Viktor E. Frankl, *Man's Search for Meaning* (Boston: Beacon Press, 2006), chap. 1, 76, Kindle.

[7] Judith Evans Grubbs and Tim Parkin, eds., *The Oxford Handbook of Childhood and Education in the Classical World* (New York: Oxford University Press, 2013), 45.

[8] Westminster Assembly, *The Westminster Confession of Faith,* Edinburgh ed. (Philadelphia: William S. Young, 1851), 387.

3. HEVEL

[1] For more on this, see: "Hevel," The Bible Project, August 28, 2017, https://bibleproject.com/podcast/ecclesiastes-part-1-hevel/.

[2] Insects Limited, "Complete Life Cycle of the Fruit Fly," YouTube, August 27, 2021, 4:25, www.youtube.com/watch?v=WJ75QeNViog.

[3] Authorship and date are debated, but I hold the author to be King Solmon in the tenth century BC.

[4] Linkin Park, "In the End," by Joseph Hahn, Brad Delson, Mike Shinoda, Robert G. Bourdon, and Chester Charles Bennington, *Hybrid Theory*, Warner Records, 2000.

5. TODDLERS

[1] ESPN, "Ice Cube reacts to the death of Kobe Bryant," *The Jump*, YouTube, January 27, 2020, 6:28, www.youtube.com/watch?v=Rd8elC_JZQo.

[2] Antonio Planas, "Man Fatally Shot in Alabama," NBC News, October 11, 2021, www.nbcnews.com/news/us-news/man-fatally-shot-alabama-after-argument-over-college-football-police-n1281287.

[3] Timothy Keller, introduction to *Counterfeit Gods: The Empty Promises of Money, Sex, and Power, and the Only Hope That Matters* (New York: Penguin Books, 2011), Kindle.

6. ZOMBIES

[1] "Why Zombies Eat Brains," Zombiepedia, accessed May 28, 2024, https://zombie.fandom.com/wiki/Why_Zombies_Eat_Brains%3F.

[2] "The Return of the Living Dead Quotes," IMDB, accessed May 28, 2024, www.imdb.com/title/tt0089907/quotes/#.

[3] Deidre McPhillips, "Overdose deaths continue to rise in the US, reaching another record level, provisional data shows," CNN, September 13, 2023, www.cnn.com/2023/09/13/health/overdose-deaths-record-april-2023/index.html.

[4] Hannah Ray Lambert, "Crisis in the Northwest: Drugs leave rural areas to rot in the shadows, 'like playing Whac-A-Mole,'" Fox News, February 10, 2024, www.foxnews.com/politics/crisis-northwest-drugs-leave-rural-areas-rot-shadows-playing-whac-mole.

[5] "SAMHSA Announces National Survey on Drug Use and Health (NSDUH) Results Detailing Mental Illness and Substance Use Levels in 2021," Substance Abuse and Mental Health Services Administration, January 4, 2023, www.samhsa.gov/newsroom/press-announcements/20230104/samhsa-announces-nsduh-results-detailing-mental-illness-substance-use-levels-2021.

[6] John Shumway, "Study finds nearly 57% of Americans admit to being addicted to their phones," CBS News, August 30, 2023, www.cbsnews.com/pittsburgh/news/study-finds-nearly-57-of-americans-admit-to-being-addicted-to-their-phones/.

[7] Harry Enten, "American happiness hits record lows," CNN, February 2, 2022, www.cnn.com/2022/02/02/politics/unhappiness-americans-gallup-analysis/index.html.

7. RELIGIOUS MATERIALIST

[1] David Foster Wallace, *This Is Water: Some Thoughts, Delivered on a Significant Occasion, about Living a Compassionate Life* (New York: Little, Brown), 2009, Kindle, 102.

[2] Sigal Samuel, "A Design Lab is Making Rituals for Secular People," *The Atlantic*, May 7, 2018, www.theatlantic.com/technology/archive/2018/05/ritual-design-lab-secular-atheist/559535/#.

[3] Samuel, "A Design Lab."

[4] Ritual Design Lab, accessed April 10, 2024, www.ritualdesignlab.org/.

[5] The Editors of Encyclopaedia Britannica, "Reign of Terror," Britannica, last updated March 29, 2025, www.britannica.com/event/Reign-of-Terror.

[6] "The French Revolution," Open Educational Resources Commons, accessed April 10, 2024, https://oercommons.org/courseware/lesson/87916/student-old/.

[7] Franklin L. Baumer, *Religion and the Rise of Scepticism* (New York: Harcourt, Brace and Company, 1960), 35.

[8] James A. Herrick, *The Making of the New Spirituality: The Eclipse of the Western Religious Tradition* (Downers Grove, IL: InterVarsity Press, 2004), 75-76.

[9] Justin Brierley, Elizabeth Oldfield, and Alex O'Connor, "Christian Revival: Fantasy or Reality," *UnHerd* (podcast), May 14, 2024, 34:50, https://unherd.com/watch-listen/christian-revival-fantasy-or-reality.

[10] Brierley, Oldfield, and O'Connor, "Christian Revival: Fantasy or Reality."

[11] See the Transcendental Argument for God.

[12] Bret Weinstein, "Russelling with God," *The DarkHorse Podcast*, May 20, 2024, https://podcasts.apple.com/us/podcast/russelling-with-god-russell-brand-on-darkhorse/id1471581521?i=1000656178469.

9. SONG

[1] Karyn O'Connor, "Anatomy of the Voice," Singwise, accessed April 29, 2024, www.singwise.com/articles/anatomy-of-the-voice.

[2] Howard E. LeWine, "Oxytocin: The Love Hormone," Harvard Health Publishing, June 13, 2023, www.health.harvard.edu/mind-and-mood/oxytocin-the-love-hormone.

[3] T Moritz Schladt, Gregory Nordmann, Roman Emilus, Brigitte Kudielka, Trynke Jong, Inga Neumann, "Choir versus Solo Singing: Effects on Mood, and Salivary Oxytocin and Cortisol Concentrations," *Frontiers in Human Neuroscience*, vol. 11 (September 14, 2017): 430, www.ncbi.nlm.nih.gov/pmc/articles/PMC5603757/.

[4] "Choral Singers Sync Heartbeats," *Scientific American*, July 8, 2013, 1:19, www.scientificamerican.com/podcast/60-second-science/choral-singers-sync-heartbeats-13-07-08/.

[5] Stuart Townend, "In Christ Alone," by Stuart Townend and Keith Getty, *Lord of Every Heart*, Integrity Music, 2002.

[6] Reginald Heber, "Holy, Holy, Holy! Lord God Almighty!" (1826), https://hymnary.org/text/holy_holy_holy_lord_god_almighty_early.

[7] Carl Gustaf Boberg, "How Great Thou Art," trans. Stuart K. Hine (1949), https://hymnary.org/text/o_lord_my_god_when_i_in_awesome_wonder.

[8] Katy Perry, "E.T.," by Max Martin, Lukasz Gottwald, Joshua Coleman, and Katy Perry, *Teenage Dream*, Capitol, 2010.

[9] Stuart Townend, "How Deep the Father's Love," *Say the Word*, Integrity Music, 1990.

[10] Stuart Townend, "In Christ Alone," by Stuart Townend and Keith Getty, *Lord of Every Heart*, Integrity Music, 2002.

[11] The hymn "Amazing Grace" by John Newton was originally published in 1779.

[12] "This Is My Father's World" was written by Maltbie Davenport Babcock and published in 1901.

[13] The hymn "Be Thou My Vision" does not have certain origins, but the lyrics have been attributed to Dallán Forgaill, written in the sixth century.

10. BAPTISM

[1] Westminster Assembly, *The Westminster Confession of Faith: Edinburgh Edition* (Philadelphia: William S. Young, 1851), 422.

[2] Tertullian, *De corona* iii, www.newadvent.org/fathers/0304.htm.

[3] Hippolytus, *The Apostolic Tradition of Hippolytus*, trans. Burton Scott Easton (Cambridge, England: Cambridge University Press, 1934), part 2, www.gutenberg.org/files/61614/61614-h/61614-h.htm.

[4] For a helpful article on renouncing the devil, see Ryan Griffith, "Have You Renounced Satan?," Desiring God, February 18, 2023, www.desiringgod.org/articles/have-you-renounced-satan#fn3.

[5] Saint Augustine, *Teaching Christianity (On Christian Doctrine)* vol. 1/2, The Works of Saint Augustine: A Translation for the 21st Century (El Segundo, CA: New City Press, 1996) Kindle 1:27.

11. COMMUNION

[1] Yes, I know . . . and grape juice too.
[2] See the prayer, "Saint Patrick's Breastplate."

12. THANKSGIVING

[1] John Anthony McGuckin, *The Eastern Orthodox Church: A New History* (New Haven, CT: Yale University Press, 2020), 28.
[2] Basil the Great, "De Spiritu Sancto," chap. 27, www.newadvent.org/fathers/3203.htm.

13. BIBLE

[1] Pliny the Elder, *The Natural History*, 21: 14.
[2] C. S. Lewis, *Surprised by Joy: The Shape of My Early Life* (New York: HarperCollins, 2017), Kindle, chap. 8.
[3] Sallustius, *On the Gods and the World*, chap. 4.

14. CHURCH

[1] James 5:16; Ephesians 5:19; Galatians 6:2; 1 Thessalonians 4:18; 1 Peter 4:9.
[2] Susan J. Jackson, "POW share their experiences so others learn," US Army Corps of Engineers, September 5, 2014, www.saj.usace.army.mil/Media/News-Stories/Article/496853/pow-share-their-experiences-so-others-learn/.
[3] For a helpful resource on this, see Jay Kim, *Analog Church* (Downers Grove, IL: InterVarsity Press, 2020).
[4] Surgeon General's Advisory, "Our Epidemic of Loneliness and Isolation: The U.S. Surgeon General's Advisory on the Healing Effects of Social Connection and Community," 2023, www.hhs.gov/sites/default/files/surgeon-general-social-connection-advisory.pdf.
[5] Dan Witters, "Loneliness in U.S. Subsides from Pandemic High," Gallup, April 4, 2023, https://news.gallup.com/poll/473057/loneliness-subsides-pandemic-high.aspx.
[6] American Psychiatric Association, "New APA Poll: One in Three Americans Feels Lonely Every Week," American Psychiatric Association, January 30, 2024, www.psychiatry.org/news-room/news-releases/new-apa-poll-one-in-three-americans-feels-lonely-e.
[7] American Psychiatric Association, "New APA Poll."
[8] Jeffrey M. Jones, "U.S. Church Membership Falls Below Majority for First Time," Gallup, March 29, 2021, https://news.gallup.com/poll/341963/church-membership-falls-below-majority-first-time.aspx.
[9] Kim Parker et al., "What Unites and Divides Urban, Suburban, and Rural Communities," Pew Research Center, May 22, 2018, www.pewresearch.org/social-trends/2018/05/22/what-unites-and-divides-urban-suburban-and-rural-communities/.

15. THE LORD'S PRAYER

[1] *Didache (Teaching of the Twelve Apostles)*, 8.3.

[2] Cyprian of Carthage, "On the Lord's Prayer," in *Fathers of the Third Century: Hippolytus, Cyprian, Novatian, Appendix*, ed. Alexander Roberts, James Donaldson, and A. Cleveland Coxe, trans. Robert Ernest Wallis, vol. 5, *The Ante-Nicene Fathers* (Buffalo, NY: Christian Literature Company, 1886), 450.

[3] One of my favorite bands has a song that beautifully illustrates this. See Citizens, "Doubting Doubts," by Adam Skatula, Brian Eichelberger, Nathan Furtado, Spencer Abbott, and Zach Bolen, *A Mirror Dimly*, Gospel Song Records, 2016.

[4] *Les Misérables*, directed by Tom Hooper (Universal Pictures, 2012).

[5] *The Wingfeather Saga*, "The Jewels of Anniera," directed by John Sanford, aired March 10, 2023, on Angel Studios.

[6] C. S. Lewis, *The Voyage of the Dawn Treader* (New York: HarperCollins, 1994), 213.

16. SPIRITS

[1] *Collins COBUILD Advanced Learner's Dictionary*, s.v. "spirit of the age," accessed April 1, 2025, www.collinsdictionary.com/us/dictionary/english/the-spirit-of-the-age-the-spirit-of-the-times.

[2] I explore this idea as it relates to social media addiction here: Isaac Serrano, "What If Our Kids Are Addicted to the Spirit of the Age?," The Gospel Coalition, July 31, 2023, www.thegospelcoalition.org/article/kids-addicted-spirit-age/.

[3] Project 86, "Necktie Remedy," by Alex Albert, Andrew Schwab, Benjamin Kaplan, Randy Torres, and Steven Dail, *And the Rest Will Follow*, Capitol Christian Music Group, 2005.

[4] For more on this see Jonathan Pageau's work on angels, principalities, spirits, cities, and egregores on his YouTube channel. For a bit of a deep dive see "Collective Intelligence: Angels in Scientific Terms | with John Vervaeke," November 26, 2021, www.youtube.com/watch?v=Y9ZaFNIH0co and "Egregors, Mobs, and Demons | with Jordan Hall and John Vervaeke," June 24, 2022, www.youtube.com/watch?v=89uP5KiP1sI.

17. THE STONE AND THE SCULPTOR

[1] Tania Lombrozo, "Do you Suffer from Illusions of Moral Superiority?," NPR, January 23, 2017, www.npr.org/sections/13.7/2017/01/23/511164613/do-you-suffer-from-illusions-of-moral-superiority.